The Life of Saint Severinus

Eugippius, George Washington Robinson

MANIBUS

GUILIELMI WATSON GOODWIN

ADAMS SHERMAN HILL

JACOBI BRADSTREET GREENOUGH

CLEMENTIS LAURENTII SMITH

ΤΩΝ ΜΑΚΑΡΙΤΩΝ

SACRUM

PREFACE

It has been said of the French, and might with equal truth be said of the Germans, that they make all excellent pieces of antiquity their own. That we are yet far from being in a position to make the same boast in behalf of our noble English tongue; that our deficiency is particularly great as respects the last centuries of ancient civilization, which have so immediate a relation to the mediaeval and modern worlds; and that in those centuries it would be difficult to find a writing more worthy of introduction to English readers than the work which Teuffel terms " the incomparable biography of Saint Severinus ": these facts, I trust, may be considered in some measure to justify the present publication.

This translation of the Life of Severinus, the first, so far as appears, in our language,[1] is from the recension of the text by Theodor Mommsen, published at Berlin, in 1898, in the series of *Scriptores Rerum Ger-*

[1] Professor Carlton H. Hayes translates Chapters I, II, VII, XX, and XL, and parts of V, VIII, and XI, in *An Introduction to the Sources relating to the Germanic Invasions* (New York, 1909), pp. 128–133. His translation seems to be made, not from the Latin text, but from the German version of Rodenberg.

manicarum. In an Appendix, pp. 117–121 below, I have given a list of editions and translations. Mommsen's preface contains an account of the manuscripts of the Life, of the chronology of the time, so far as it casts direct light upon the careers of Severinus and Eugippius, and of the references to Eugippius and Severinus in later ecclesiastical writers.[1] One who desires a more general view of the period may obtain it by reading the pertinent chapters of Hodgkin, Dahn, or Gibbon, or Julius von Pflugk-Harttung's *The Great Migrations*, which, translated from the *Allgemeine Weltgeschichte*, forms the sixth volume in Wright's *History of All Nations*. Passages referring specifically to Severinus may be found in Pflugk-Harttung's volume, in the English translation, on pages 250 f., 269, and 296. Julius Jung, in his *Römer und Romanen in den Donauländern* (Innsbruck, 1877),[2] pages 133–141, 150–156, etc., discusses the Life with particular reference to the light which it sheds upon the ethnography and local history of Noricum and the adjacent provinces. I will also mention the paragraphs on

---

[1] Mommsen does not mention the passage in the biography of Willibald, the Saxon pilgrim, who visited Naples in 729. "Et ibi est prope castella [*sic*] ubi requiescit sanctus Severinus." *Vita Willibaldi*, 4, in *Monumenta Germaniae Historica*, Scriptores, xv, 1 (1887).

[2] In the second edition (Innsbruck, 1887) much of the material relative to the Life is omitted.

Eugippius in Teuffel and Schwabe's *History of Roman Literature* (Warr's translation, London, 1900), section 494, and in Adolf Ebert's *Geschichte der Christlich-lateinischen Literatur bis zum Zeitalter Karls des Grossen* (Leipsic, 1874), pp. 431 ff., and the somewhat longer passage in Albert Hauck's *Kirchengeschichte Deutschlands*, vol. i (Leipsic, 1887), pp. 328–331.

André Baudrillart's *Saint Séverin* (1908), in the series *Les Saints*, and *Die Lebensbeschreibung Severins als kulturgeschichtliche Quelle* (1903), by Theo Sommerlad, require no more than passing notice.

Matthaeus Rader's *Bavaria Sancta* contains spirited engravings by Raphael Sadeler, one of which represents the night scene where Severinus recalls the priest Silvinus from the dead.

Mention may be made of two popular accounts of Severinus for English readers: Alban Butler's in *The Lives of the Fathers, Martyrs, and other Principal Saints* (London, 1812–13), vol. i, pp. 113 ff; and Charles Kingsley's in *The Hermits* (London, 1869), pp. 224–239, with a translation of Chapter VIII. Sabine Baring-Gould, after excising all passages of Kingsley's essay that could offend the most credulous, reprints the remainder in *The Lives of the Saints* (London, 1872–77), vol. i, pp. 101–112.

The most recent German translations of the Life are by Karl Rodenberg (Leipsic, 1878, second edition, 1884), in *Geschichtschreiber der deutschen Vorzeit*, and by Sebastian Brunner (Vienna, 1879).

I thank heartily for courteous assistance Dr. Gennaro Aspreno Galante of Naples, who has given me invaluable help, particularly as respects the recent history of the remains of Severinus; Professor James Hardy Ropes of Harvard University; Professor Cesare Barone, First Archivist of the Royal Neapolitan State Archives; and Librarian Professor Ferdinand Ludwig Schmidt, Dr. Edward D. Snyder, and Mr. Julius Klein, who have kindly examined for me in the Royal Public Library at Dresden, the British Museum, and the Bibliothèque Nationale at Paris several editions and translations not accessible in Cambridge.

GEORGE W. ROBINSON.

CAMBRIDGE, MASSACHUSETTS,
July, 1914.

CONTENTS

LETTER OF EUGIPPIUS TO PASCHASIUS

To the holy and venerable Deacon Paschasius, Eugippius sends his salutation in Christ.

About two years ago, in the consulship of Importunus,[1] a letter of a noble layman, directed to a priest, was offered me to read. It contained the life of Bassus a monk, who formerly dwelt in the monastery of the mountain called Titas, above Ariminum, and later died in the district of Lucania: a man very well known to me and to many others. When I learned that some were making copies of this letter, I began to reflect, and also to declare to the clergy, that the great miracles which the divine power had wrought through Saint Severinus ought not to be hidden.

When the author of the letter knew of this, he eagerly requested me to send him some memoranda in regard to Saint Severinus, that he might write a short account of the saint's life for the benefit of later generations. In response to this offer, I prepared a memoir, filled full with testimonies from the daily narrations of the elder brethren, with which I was perfectly familiar. Yet I did this with great regret; for I deemed it unreasonable, that, while thou wert alive, I should ask a layman to write a life of Severinus. It

[1] A.D. 509.

seemed rash to impose upon a lay writer the arrangement and composition of the work. Cultivated in profane literature alone, he would be likely to compose the biography in a style difficult for many to understand; so that the remarkable events, which had too long remained hidden in silence and night, might fail through the obscurity of his eloquence to shine brightly forth for us, untrained as we are in polite letters.

But I shall search no more for the feeble light of that lamp now that thy sun-like radiance is here. Only veil not the rays of thy knowledge by a cloud of excuse, accusing thine own ignorance. Lash me not, I beseech thee, with harsh terms; say not, Why expect water from the flint ? Indeed I do not expect water from the flint of this world's highway, but from thee, who, comparing spiritual things with spiritual,[1] shalt refresh us from the living rock by that honey of speech with which thou overflowest; and already from that honey thou sendest a nectar-taste of sweetest promise, while thou biddest me transmit a memoir or notes upon the life of Saint Severinus.

Until these memoranda win admission to a book of thy construction, let them not offend the mind of the critic. For he who seeks an architect to build a house, carefully prepares the necessary materials; but if the architect delays, and he puts together in the likeness of walls unfashioned heaps from the rough stones, ought one to speak of his work as a building,

---

[1] I Corinthians, ii, 13.

when no master has constructed, and no proper foundation has been laid? So I, who have with difficulty prepared and most miserably put together the precious material for thy genius, ought I to be thought to have composed what I desire, when a liberal education has not fashioned the work, nor literary training lent it elevation and elegance? My work has, indeed, the sure foundation of faith alone; that foundation upon which, as thou knowest, rose the saint's admirable, resplendent virtues; and now I commit the materials to the architect, whose hands shall be thy eloquence; and when the capstone is placed upon thy work, I shall return due thanks to Christ.

I beg that thou have the goodness to mention also those miraculous cures, which, either on the journey or here, were wrought by divine virtue unto the memory of the blessed father Severinus. Since the trusty bearer, thy son Deogratias, best knows these, I have entrusted to him to communicate them to thee by word of mouth. And I hope that I may speedily be able yet again to call him bearer on the completion of thy work; that so this most faithful servant of God, rich in such great virtues, while he is carried to the glory of the saints by his merits vouchsafed through Christ's grace may by thy pen be immortalized to human memory.

It may perhaps be asked, and with justice, from what country Severinus sprang; since with this particular it is the custom to begin the story of any life. I

confess I have no clear evidence. For many priests
and clerics, and lords temporal and spiritual, natives
of the country or drawn together to him from afar,
often debated the nationality of this man of such great
and resplendent virtue. And they were at a loss, but
no one ventured to question him directly. There was,
however, a certain Primenius, a noble priest of Italy,
and a man of the highest standing, who had fled to
him for refuge at the time when the patrician Orestes [1]
was unjustly slain. This man, it was said, had been
like a father to Orestes, and therefore feared his
murderers. He, then, having won the saint's friendship, and enjoyed it for many days, served as spokes-
man for the rest, and burst out with the question.
" Reverend master," he said, " from what province
hath the great light come,[2] which God hath seen fit to
bestow upon these lands ? " The man of God first
answered him with a cheerful jest, " If thou thinkest
me a fugitive slave,[3] prepare a ransom which thou
canst offer for me when I am claimed." Presently he
added, more seriously, " What profiteth it the servant
of God to name his country or race, when by keeping

---

[1] Orestes was by birth a Roman provincial of Pannonia. Priscus
(Bonnae, 1829), pp. 146, 185; Jordanes, *De Rebus Geticis*, 45; Anonymus Valesianus, 38.

[2] J. H. von Falckenstein neatly expands the metaphor in his ap-
preciation of Severinus. *Geschichten des grossen Herzogthums und
ehemaligen Königreichs Bayern* (Munich, etc., 1763), i, p. 78.

[3] *Fugitivus*. For the Roman law in regard to fugitive slaves and
their recovery, one may consult W. W. Buckland, *The Roman Law of
Slavery* (Cambridge, England, 1908), pp. 267–274, and the *Codex Theo-
dosianus*, x, 12, *Si vagum petatur mancipium*.

them silent he can more easily avoid vainglory ?[1]
For vainglory is like the left hand, without whose
knowledge[2] he desireth through the gift of Christ to
accomplish every good work; that so he may deserve
to be among those on Christ's right hand,[3] and to be
enrolled as a citizen of the celestial country.   And if
thou knowest that I, though unworthy, truly desire
that celestial country, what need that thou learn the
earthly country of which thou askest ?   But know
that the same God who called thee to the priesthood,
commanded me also to minister unto these perilled
folk."   The answer silenced Primenius, nor did any
one before or after presume to question the saint upon
this matter.

Yet his speech revealed a man of purest Latin stock;
and it is understood that he first departed into some
desert place of the East because of his fervid desire
for a more perfect life, and that thence, constrained by
divine revelation, he later came to the towns of Riverside Noricum, near Upper Pannonia, which were
harassed by frequent incursions of the barbarians.   So
he himself was wont to hint, in obscure language as if
speaking of another, naming some cities of the East,
and indicating that he had passed by miracle through
the dangers of an immense journey.[4]

---

[1] " Quo ipso non obscure indicabat, magno se ortu, et cujus indi-
cium jactantiae serviret."   Marcus Hansitz, *Germania Sacra* (Augustae Vindelicorum, etc., 1727–55), i, p. 80.

[2] Matthew, vi, 3.   [3] Matthew, xxv, 33.

[4] The detailed account of the early life of Severinus, given in Theo
Sommerlad's *Die Lebensbeschreibung Severins als kulturgeschichtliche*

Even in the lifetime of Saint Severinus, I never heard other particulars in regard to his native place than those I have related. The testimonies concerning his marvellous life accompany this letter, arranged as a memoir, with a table of chapters prefixed. Grant my request, and let them gain greater fame through thy editorial care.[1] It remains to ask that thou cease not to associate thy prayers with his for the pardon of my sins.

Quelle, pp. 62–68, needs mention only by way of caution. Sommerlad carries ingenuity to a great excess.

[1] "It is exceedingly doubtful whether the request was seriously meant. Similar expressions are very common, which are no more than polite phrases." Wilhelm Wattenbach, *Deutschlands Geschichtsquellen im Mittelalter* (6th ed., Berlin, 1893–94), i, p. 49.

TABLE OF CHAPTERS

[1] The place names in the ablative form, Asturis, Comagenis, Favianis, etc., mark the tendency of the provincial Latin to develop into Romance dialects.

THE
LIFE OF SAINT SEVERINUS

CHAPTER I

At the time of the death of Attila, king of the Huns,[1] confusion reigned in the two Pannonias and the other borderlands of the Danube. Then Severinus, most holy servant of God, came from the parts of the East to the marches of Riverside Noricum [2] and the Pannonias, and tarried in a little town which is called Asturis.[3] There he lived in accordance with the evangelical and apostolic doctrine, in all piety and chastity, in the confession of the Catholic faith, and fulfilled his reverend purpose by holy works. By such exercises strengthened, he innocently sought the crown of the celestial calling; and one day, as was his wont, went forth to the church. Then the priests, the clergy, and the citizens were fetched, and he began in all humility of mind to prophesy, how they ought to

---

[1] In 453.

[2] *Noricum Ripense.* Rodenberg renders by the German equivalent, *Ufernoricum.* In the translation of Professor Hayes, *Ufernoricum*, both here and in Chapter XI, becomes ' Upper Noricum,' which is not a happy guess.

[3] Probably on the site of the present Klosterneuburg, a little above Vienna.

ward off the threatening snares of the enemy by
prayers, and by fastings, and by the fruits of compassion.   But their stubborn hearts, defiled by fleshly
lusts, proved the oracles of the prophet by the decision
of their unbelief.   Yet the servant of God returned to
the lodging where the sacristan [1] of the church had
received him, and made known the day and hour of
imminent destruction.   " I go in haste," he said,
" from a stubborn town that shall swiftly perish."

Then he went away to the next town, which is called
Comagenis.[2]   This was very strictly guarded by the
barbarians established within, who had entered into
a league [3] with the Romans, and it was not easy for
any one to secure permission to go in or to leave.   Yet,
though they knew him not, they neither questioned
the servant of God, nor turned him back.   So anon he
went into the church; and when he found all in despair

---

[1] *Custos.* The office is not to be confounded with that of janitor
or doorkeeper (*ostiarius*) mentioned in Chapters X and XVI, below.
Isidorus Hispalensis, *De Ecclesiasticis Officiis*, ii, 9, says: " Custodes
sacrarii, Levitae sunt.   Ipsis enim jussum est custodire tabernaculum,
et omnia vasa templi . . . praeferentes speciem gravitatis."   In his
Regula Monachorum, 20, he describes somewhat more fully the duties
of the position in a monastery church: " Ad custodem sacrarii
pertinet cura vel custodia templi, signum quoque dandi in vespertinis
nocturnisque officiis; vela, vestesque sacrae, ac vasa sacrorum,
codices quoque instrumentaque cuncta, oleum in usum sanctuarii,
cera et luminaria."

[2] Near Tulln.

[3] A euphemism.   Marcus Velserus justly remarks, " Quam misera
et deplorata illis temporibus harum provinciarum fuerit conditio, ex
uno isto foedere satis superque colligi poterat, nisi reliqua omnia in
id argumentum conspiraret."   *Opera* (Norimbergae, 1682), p. 667.

of their safety, he exhorted them to be armed with
fasting and prayers and almsgivings, and set forth
examples of salvation from of old, in which the protection of God had freed his people in unforeseen and
wondrous ways.   And when they hesitated to believe
one who at the very crisis of peril promised the safety
of all, the old man came who at Asturis had long been
the host of Severinus (how great a guest!).   When the
guards at the gates anxiously questioned the old man,
his deportment and words revealed the destruction of
his town.   He added that it was destroyed on the
same day that a certain man of God had foretold.
When they heard this, they eagerly replied, " Thinkest
thou he is the same, who in our despair promises us the
assistance of God ? "   Then straightway the old man
recognized the servant of God within the church, and
cast himself at his feet, saying that through his kind-
ness he had been spared the destruction which had
overtaken his townsmen.

CHAPTER II

WHEN they had heard these things, the inhabitants of
Comagenis begged forgiveness for their unbelief, and
obeyed with holy works the admonitions of the man of
God.   They made a fast, and assembled in the church
for the space of three days, reproaching their past sins
with groans and lamentations.   But on the third day,
during the celebration of the evening sacrifice, there

was a sudden earthquake;[1] and the barbarians who
dwelt within the city were so terrorsmitten that they
compelled the Romans to open the gates for them in
haste. Then they rushed out tumultuously, and
scattered, supposing themselves besieged and surrounded by near foes; and their terror was augmented
by divine influence, so that, in the wanderings and
confusion of the night, they slew one another with the
sword. Thus utter destruction consumed the enemy;
and the people, saved by the divine aid, learned
through the saint to fight with heavenly arms.

[1] I think it probable that this is the earthquake mentioned in
Anonymus Cuspiniani, *Chronicon* (in Thomas Roncallius, *Vetustiora
Chronica*, Patavii, 1787, ii, col. 124) under the year 455: " eversa est
Sabaria a Terraemotu VII. idus septemb. die Veneris "; and in the
same words, and under the same year, in the *Excerptum Sangallense*
(in Karl Frick, *Chronica Minora*, vol. 1, 1892, p. 422). Sabaria was
in Upper Pannonia, about seventy miles southeast of Comagenis in a
straight line, or ninety-two Roman miles by road. *Antonini Augusti
Itinerarium*, pp. 233 f. Wesseling.

The date of this earthquake as given in the chronicles clearly cannot be correct. The Friday before the Ides fell, in September 455, on
the 9th, not on the 7th. I suggest accordingly that, following
C. F. Roesler (*Chronica Medii Aevi*, Tubingae, 1798, i, p. 341),
we make the obvious emendation, and read " V. idus Septembres die
Veneris." Theodor Mommsen (*Chronica Minora*, Berlin, 1892–98, i,
p. 304; in *Monumenta Germaniae Historica*) suggests the reading
" IV.," " nisi in anno erratum est "; but he cannot be right. One
might, it is true, reach his result by using inadvertently a table like
that in Sir Harris Nicolas's *The Chronology of History* (London, 1835),
p. 49, which contains the dominical letters for 4000 years after the
Christian era, according to the New Style. The New Style, however,
does not apply to the fifth century.

CHAPTER III

AT the same time a cruel famine had prostrated a city named Favianis,[1] and the inhabitants believed that their only remedy would be by devout prayers to invite the man of God from the town of Comagenis. He foreknew that they would come to him, and was moved by the Lord to go with them. When he had come thither, he began to exhort the people of the city, saying, " By the fruits of repentance ye shall be able to be freed from so great a calamity of hunger." While they were profiting by such instructions, most blessed Severinus learned by divine revelation that a certain widow, Procula by name, had concealed much produce of the fields. He called her before the people, and vehemently rebuked her. " Daughter of most noble parents," he said, " why dost thou make thyself the handmaid of avarice and stand forth the slave of covetousness, which is, as the apostle teaches, idolatry ?[2] Lo, the Lord in his compassion hath regard for his servants; and thou shalt not have any use for thine ill-gotten wealth, except to cast into the stream of the Danube the corn too long withheld, and so to exhibit to fishes the humanity which thou hast

---

[1] On the Danube between Tulln and Lorch; perhaps near the site of the present town of Mautern.

[2] Colossians, iii, 5; Ephesians, v, 5. Of these passages the former is of course the one to which direct reference is made. Bolland, Sauppe, Rodenberg, Knoell, and Mommsen, all have followed Surius in giving only the reference to Ephesians, which is purely secondary.

denied to men! Wherefore aid thyself rather than the poor from those things which thou yet thinkest to keep, while Christ hungers." [1] When she·heard these sayings, the woman was filled with great fear and trembling; and began willingly to expend her hoards for the poor.

Not long after, there unexpectedly appeared at the bank of the Danube a vast number of boats from the Raetias, laden with great quantities of merchandise, which had been hindered for many days by the thick ice of the river Aenus.[2] When at last God's command had loosed the ice, they brought down an abundance of food to the famine-stricken. Then all began to praise God with uninterrupted devotion, as the bestower of unhoped relief; for they had expected to perish, wasted by the long famine, and they acknowledged that manifestly the boats had come out of due season, loosed from the ice and frost by the prayers of the servant of God.[3]

[1] Matthew, xxv, 35–42; Salvian, *Adversus Avaritiam*, iv, 4: " Christus . . . cum esurientibus esurit . . . quid ais, o homo, qui Christianum te esse dicis, . . . Christus esurit, et tu delitias affluentibus paras ? "

[2] The Inn.

[3] " Calidis Severini precibus solutae." Andreas Brunner, *Annalium Boicorum Partes III* (ed. nova, Francofurti ad Moenum, 1710), col. 118.

CHAPTER IV

At the same time barbarian robbers made an unexpected plundering incursion, and led away captive all the men and cattle they found without the walls. Then many of the citizens flocked weeping to the man of God, recounted to him the destructive calamity that had come upon them, and showed him evidences of the recent rapine.

But he straitly questioned Mamertinus, then a tribune, who afterwards was ordained bishop, whether he had with him any armed men with whom to institute an energetic pursuit of the robbers. Mamertinus replied, " I have soldiers, a very few. But I dare not contend with such a host of enemies. However, if thou commandest it, venerable father, though we lack the aid of weapons yet we believe that through thy prayers we shall be victorious." And the servant of God said, " Even if thy soldiers are unarmed, they shall now be armed from the enemy. For neither numbers nor fleshly courage is required, when everything proves that God is our champion. Only in the name of the Lord advance swiftly, advance confidently. For when God in his compassion goes before, the weakest shall seem the bravest. The Lord shall fight for you,[1] and ye shall be silent. Then make haste; and this one thing observe above everything, to conduct unharmed into my presence those of the barbarians whom thou shalt take."

[1] Exodus, xiv, 14.

Then they went forth.   At the second milestone, by
a brook which is called Tiguntia, they came upon the
foe.   Some of the robbers escaped by hasty flight,
abandoning their weapons.   The soldiers bound the
rest and brought them captive to the servant of God,
as he had commanded.   He freed them from chains,
refreshed them with food and drink, and briefly addressed them.   " Go," he said, " and command your
confederates not to dare to approach this place again
in their lust for booty.   For the judgment and retri-
bution of heaven shall straightway punish them, since
God fights for his servants, whom his supernal power
is wont so to protect that hostile missiles do not inflict
wounds upon them, but rather furnish them with
arms."   Then the barbarians were sent away; and he
rejoiced over the miracles of Christ, and promised
that through Christ's compassion Favianis should
have no further experience of hostile pillage; only let
neither prosperity nor adversity withdraw the citizens
from the work of God.

Then Saint Severinus withdrew into a more remote
spot, which was called Ad Vineas, where a small cell
contented him.[1]   But he was compelled by a divine
revelation to return to Favianis;[2] so that, though the

[1] Georg Kaufmann says, " Seine Wohnung war eine Zelle, oft auch
eine Höhle." *Deutsche Geschichte bis auf Karl den Grossen* (Leipsic,
1880–81), ii, p. 25.   I find this cavern only in Kaufmann's work.

[2] Favianis was long identified with Vienna by an erroneous tradi-
tion.   Joannes Cuspinianus, the great sixteenth century scholar,
believed that his estate in the suburbs of Vienna comprised Ad Vineas
and the cell of Severinus. *Austria* (Francofurti, 1601), pp. 55, 69:

quiet of his cell was dear to him, he yet obeyed the commands of God and built a monastery not far from the city.[1] There he began to instruct great numbers in the sacred way of life, training the souls of his hearers rather by deeds than by words.[2] He often

"Villam enim S. Severini, ubi cellam habuit pius pater S. Severinus, jam ego possideo, ubi nobilissima crescunt vineta, arboribus illic desectis ac purgatis. . . . a sancto Severino patria lingua Severin appellatur."

Cuspinianus calls Severinus " second apostle of Austria " (*secundarius Austriae apostolus, alter Australium apostolus*), the first being Quirinus, and reckons him among the six patron saints of that country: the martyrs Quirinus, Maximilian, Florian; Severinus; Colman the Irish pilgrim; Margrave Leopold III the Pious. On p. 70 of his *Austria* is printed a poem by Joannes Stabius, " In Sanctos Austriae Patronos Precatio," in forty-six hexameter verses. The poem contains, however, nothing which seems to have individual reference to Severinus, unless it be in vv. 32–38:

"Praesidio semper secura sit Austria vestro.
Morborum omne genus, quae corpora nostra fatigant,
Infandumque malum, crudelem avertite pestem.
Sit flavae Cereris, laeti sit copia Bacchi:
Tartareo sonitu reboent nec classica Martem,
Sed Pax alma ferens ramum felicis olivae
Illustret terras, soror et Concordia mitis."

[1] It will be noted that the monasteries founded by Saint Severinus were in the immediate neighborhood of cities. F. W. Rettberg calls attention to this fact, and to its accordance with the monastic rule of Saint Basil the Great: with which, he suggests, Severinus may have become familiar during his wanderings in the Orient. *Kirchengeschichte Deutschlands* (Göttingen, 1846–48), i, p. 231. Compare E. C. Butler's article " Basilian Monks," in the *Encyclopaedia Britannica* (11th ed.).

[2] Wolfgang Lazius, using a singular figure, says that " from this monastery, as if from the Trojan horse, went forth almost all the bishops of Noricum." *Vienna Austriae* (Basileae, 1546), p. 54. Lazius

withdrew, indeed, to a solitary habitation, called by
the neighbors Burgum, a mile from Favianis, that he
might avoid the throngs of men that kept coming to
him, and cleave to God in uninterrupted prayer. But
the more he desired to inhabit solitude, the more was
he warned by frequent revelations not to deny his
presence to the afflicted peoples.

And so day by day his merit grew, and the fame of
his virtues increased, and this spread far and wide,
and was extended by the marks of celestial favor con-
ferred upon him. For good things cannot be concealed,
since, according to the words of the Saviour, neither
can a candle be concealed under a bushel, nor a city
that is set on a hill be hid.[1]

Among the other great gifts which the Saviour had
bestowed upon him stood out the gift of abstinence.
He subdued his flesh by innumerable fasts, teaching
that the body, if nourished with too abundant food,
will straightway bring destruction upon the soul. He
wore no shoes whatever. So at midwinter, which in
those regions is a time of cruel, numbing cold, he gave
a remarkable proof of endurance by being always will-
ing to walk barefoot. A well-known proof of the
terrible cold is afforded by the Danube, which is often
so solidly frozen by the fierce frost that it affords a
secure crossing even for carts.[2] Yet he whom the

gives a list of these bishops, which Marcus Hansitz handles very
roughly. *Germania Sacra*, i, pp. 74, 85 ff.

[1] Matthew, v, 14, 15.

[2] Jordanes (*De Rebus Geticis*, 55) says that the Danube " freezes

grace of God had elevated by such virtues was wont
to make acknowledgment with utmost humility, and
to say, " Think not that what ye see is of my merit.
It is rather an example for your salvation.   Let the
foolhardiness of man cease.   Let the pride of exalta-
tion be restrained.   That we can do anything good,
we are chosen; as the apostle [1] saith, ' He hath chosen
us before the foundation of the world, that we should
be holy and without blame before him.' [2]   Pray rather
in my behalf that the gifts of the Saviour to me may
serve not for greater condemnation, but for increase of

so hard that it will support like a solid rock an army of infantry, and
carts and sleds, or whatsoever vehicles there may be."

It is probable that modern regulation of the current of the Danube
by engineering works has had a tendency to prevent the formation of
extensive ice fields.   Yet even now the stream is frozen annually in
Lower Hungary throughout several long stretches, which at the height
of the frost can occasionally be crossed with carts or sleds.   In Bavaria, Austria, and Rumania, field ice does not form every winter.
Yet it sometimes happens even at Vienna — most recently in January, 1901 — that the ice is strong enough to allow foot travellers
a safe passage across the river.

I am indebted to the Imperial-Royal Central Bureau of Hydro-
graphy at Vienna for the information contained in the above paragraph.   One may consult also Anton Swarowsky's essay *Die Eisver-
hältnisse der Donau in Bayern und Österreich von 1850-90*, in *Geograph-
ische Abhandlungen*, edited by Albrecht Penck, Band v, Heft 1
(Vienna and Olmütz, 1891); and, for notices of the great frosts of 821
and 1076-77, Fritz Curschmann's *Hungersnöte im Mittelalter* (Leipsic,
1900), pp. 94, 121.

[1] It may be noted that in Eugippius the expression ' the apostle '
always refers to Saint Paul.   Eugippius never bestows upon Severinus the appellation ' apostle of Noricum ' (*apostolus Norici* or *apostolus Noricorum*), later so common.

[2] Ephesians, i, 4.

justification." This and the like he was wont to declare, weeping. Thus he taught men humility by his wondrous example. Standing on the secure foundation of this virtue, he shone with so great a splendor of the divine gift that even the very enemies of the church, the heretics, honored him with most reverent courtesy.

CHAPTER V

THE king of the Rugii, Flaccitheus,[1] began to feel himself unsteady on the throne at the very commencement of his reign. The Goths in Lower Pannonia were violently hostile to him, and he was alarmed by their innumerable multitude. Therefore in his perils he asked counsel of most blessed Severinus as of a heavenly oracle. Once he came to him in exceeding confusion, and declared with tears that he had asked of the princes of the Goths a passage to Italy, and

[1] A genealogical table of the Rugian royal house may be of service. Numerals in parentheses refer to the chapters in which the individuals are mentioned.

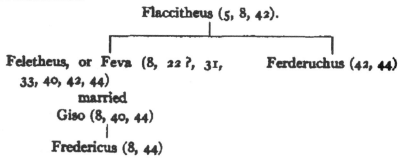

Flaccitheus (5, 8, 42).

Feletheus, or Feva (8, 22 ?, 31, 33, 40, 42, 44)
married
Giso (8, 40, 44)

Fredericus (8, 44)

Ferderuchus (42, 44)

Feba, named in Chapter XXII, is probably the same as Feletheus, or Feva.

that, as they had denied this request, he did not doubt
that they would put him to death. Then Flaccitheus
received this reply from the man of God: " If the one
Catholic faith united us, thou oughtest rather to consult me concerning eternal life;[1] but since thou art

---

[1] A comparison of this passage with the reference, in Chapter VIII,
to Queen Giso's attempt " to rebaptize certain Catholics," makes it
evident that the Rugii, or at least their sovereigns, were, like most of
the converted Germans of the fifth century and even later, Christians
of the Arian sect. The fact that the Rugii were Arians while the provincials were Catholics coöperated with the difference of race to produce a lack of complete sympathy and understanding between them.
On the other hand, it was entirely natural that the Rugii, as Christians, should assume the position towards the provincials that we find
them occupying more and more, of protectors against the depredations
of the German tribes that remained heathen: Alamanni and Thuringi
(Chapter XXXI, below, etc.); Heruli (Chapter XXIV); no doubt
also the Franks and Saxons, whom Ennodius (*De Vita Beati Antoni*,
12–14) names in connection with the Heruli as devastators of the
Pannonias during the ninth decade of the fifth century — cruel as
wild beasts; turning a populous land into a desert; worshipping gods
who, they believed, could be propitiated only by human victims;
slaughtering clerics by preference, as the sacrifices most acceptable to
their divinities.

Dr. Julius von Pflugk-Harttung's vividly worded description of life
in Noricum in the time of Severinus (*Allgemeine Weltgeschichte*, iv,
p. 231) is somewhat confusing, because of his failure to point out
clearly this distinctive position of the Rugii. He says, " They and
their neighbor-tribes, Thuringi, Heruli, Alamanni, and Goths, came
from beyond the Danube in uninterrupted forays." There is no mention in the Life of ' forays ' on the part of the Rugii, except in the
strictly technical sectarian sense of the confiscation of the monastery
plate and furniture (Chapter XLIV) ; on the contrary, they themselves suffered from plundering raids, as the next paragraph shows.
Dr. Pflugk-Harttung's reference to the Goths (Ostrogoths) is also not
to the point. They lived, not beyond the Danube but in Pannonia,
on the Roman side of the river (Jordanes, *De Rebus Geticis*, 50). Fur-

anxious only over present safety, which is of common concern to us both, hear my instruction. Be not troubled by the multitude of the Goths or by their enmity. They shall soon depart and leave thee secure, and thou shalt reign in the prosperity which thou hast desired. Only do not neglect the warnings of my humility. Let it not irk thee to seek peace even with the least; never lean upon thine own strength. 'Cursed be the man,' saith the Scripture, 'that trusteth in man, and maketh flesh his arm, and whose heart departeth from the Lord.'[1] Learn therefore to beware of snares, not to lay them: and thou shalt die in thy bed [2] with a peaceful end."

ther, they were Christians, partially civilized, and usually in alliance with the Romans against their barbarian enemies. After the death of Attila there appears to have been only one period, comprising a few months of the year 473, in which the Ostrogoths were hostile to the Western Empire (*ibid.*, 56). It is to that time that we may very reasonably assign their attack upon Tiburnia in Noricum Mediterraneum (Chapter XVII).

It is regrettable that *The Cambridge Medieval History*, i (1911) repeats the false view of the position of the Rugii. Mr. Ernest Barker, the writer of chapter xiv therein, "Italy and the West, 410-476," says (p. 420) " The Rugii . . . appear in the history of the time . . . as vexing with their inroads the parts of Noricum which lay immediately south of the river. The Life of Saint Severinus . . . describes their depredations "; and again (p. 425), " Parallel in some ways to the position of Marcellinus and Aegidius is the beneficent theocracy which Saint Severinus established about the same time in Noricum, a masterless province unprotected by Rome, and harassed by the raids of the Rugii from the north of the river."

[1] Jeremiah, xvii, 5.

[2] *In lectulo tuo.* Rodenberg renders *auf deinem Lager:* Professor Hayes has " in thine own camp."

As Flaccitheus, encouraged by this oracle, was joyfully departing, a message was brought to him that a
band of plundering barbarians had taken captive
some of the Rugii. Straightway he sent to the man
of God to ask his counsel. Severinus, by revelation of
the Lord, forewarned Flaccitheus with holy exhortations not to follow the robbers. " If thou follow them,"
he said, " thou wilt be slain. Take heed; cross not
the stream; be not taken unawares and overcome by
the triple ambush which has been prepared for thee!
For speedily a trusty messenger will come, who shall
inform thee concerning all these matters." Then
two of the captives, fleeing from the camp of the
enemy, related in order those things which the most
blessed man had foretold by revelation of Christ.
So the hostile ambush came to naught, and Flaccitheus was prospered more and more, and ended his
days in peace and tranquillity.

CHAPTER VI

Now after this one of the Rugii suffered incredible
pain from gout for twelve years, and lost all use of his
limbs. His intolerable torments were so long continued that they became well known to the neighbors
on every side. So at last, when divers remedies
availed nothing, his mother, a widow, put her son in a
cart, and having brought him to the saint, laid him
down in his desperate sickness at the door of the

monastery, and prayed with many tears that her only son might be restored to her whole.

But the man of God, perceiving that great things were demanded of him, and moved by her weeping, said: " Why am I oppressed by a deceitful fancy ? Why am I thought to be able to do what I cannot ? I have no power to accomplish such great things. Yet I give my judgment as one that hath obtained mercy of God." [1]   Then he charged the woman that she should bestow something upon the poor, according to her power.   Without delay she quickly took off the clothing which she wore, and was hastening to divide it among the needy.   When the man of God heard this, he marvelled at her ardor, and again charged her that she should clothe herself with her garments. " When thy son," he said, " has been healed by the Lord and goes with thee, then shalt thou fulfill thy vows."

So he set a fast of a few days, as was his wont, and poured forth prayers to God; and straightway healed the sick man, and sent him home whole, walking without aid.

Afterwards, when the man was present at the crowded weekly market, he exhibited the miracle, and astounded all who saw him.   For some said, " Look, it is he, whose whole body was dissolved in corruption "; while as others absolutely denied that it was he, a friendly contention arose.

---

[1] I Corinthians, vii, 25.

Now from that time when health was restored to the man who had been thought incurable, the whole nation of the Rugii resorted to the servant of God, and began to render grateful obedience, and to ask help for their diseases. Likewise many of other races, to which the fame of so great a miracle had come, desired to see the soldier of Christ.[1] With the same reverence, even before this event, some barbarians, on their way to Italy, turned aside with a view to gaining his benediction.

CHAPTER VII

AMONG such visitants was Odoacer, later king of Italy, then a tall youth, meanly clad. While he stood, stooping that his head might not touch the roof of the lowly cell, he learned from the man of God that he was to win renown. For as the young man bade him

---

[1] Adolf Harnack discusses the early conceptions of the Christian religion as a warfare, and of the Church as a military organization, in the first part of his essay *Militia Christi* (Tübingen, 1905). An illustration of the length to which these conceptions might be carried is afforded by the biography of a disciple of Severinus, Ennodius's *De Vita Beati Antoni*. Antonius, ' warrior of Christ,' decides to forsake his Alpine hermitage and to join the ' regiment of the isle Lerina' (see note to Chapter XLIV, below) of ' the army of the saints.' " That veteran battle-line is ever watchful, and repulses the enemy, after transfixing him with many blows. They number their triumphs by the wars which the devil wages against them. They are not afraid, when the shrill battle-trumpet announces Satan's onset, and urges to the fight. Daily combat ever makes soldiers skilled and brave, while a long peace relaxes them."

farewell, " Go forth ! " said Severinus, " Go forth to
Italy! Now clad in wretched hides, thou shalt soon
distribute rich gifts to many."

CHAPTER VIII

KING Feletheus, sometimes called Feva, son of Flaccitheus, mentioned above, imitated his father's diligence, and before the commencement of his reign began
to make frequent visits to the saint. His wife, Giso by
name, a dangerous and wicked woman,[1] always drew
him back from the healing works of mercy. Among
the other pollutions of her iniquity, she even attemp-
ted to rebaptize certain Catholics.[2] But when her
husband, out of his reverence for Saint Severinus, did
not consent, she incontinently abandoned her sacrilegious purpose. Yet she oppressed the Romans
with a heavy hand, and even ordered some to be
removed beyond the Danube. For one day she came
to a village near Favianis, and commanded that certain
ones should be brought to her across the Danube to
be condemned to the most degrading offices of slavery.
The man of God sent to her and asked that she let
them go. But she, her woman's anger kindled to a
white heat, replied with a message of the greatest

---

[1] Max Büdinger offers some excellent remarks on Giso's strongly
marked character. *Oesterreichische Geschichte* (Leipsic, 1858), i, p. 49.

[2] " Ausa etiam Catholico ritu ablutos, sacrilego Arianorum fonte
denuo lustrare." Johann Adlzreitter, *Annalium Boicae Gentis Partes
III* (ed. nova, Francofurti ad Moenum, 1710), col. 120.

rudeness. "Pray for thyself," she said, "servant of God, lurking in thy cell! Leave me to issue concerning my servants such orders as I please."

When the man of God received this answer, he said, "I put my trust in the Lord Jesus Christ. She shall be compelled by necessity to do that which her perverse inclination has despised."

Even so the swift stroke followed which cast down her haughty spirit. For there were certain goldsmiths, barbarians, shut up and straitly guarded that they might fashion ornaments for the king and queen. On the same day on which the queen had spurned the servant of God, the little son of King Feletheus, Fredericus by name, moved by childish curiosity, went in among them. Then the goldsmiths put a sword at the child's breast, saying that if any one should attempt to approach them without the safeguard of an oath, they would first run through the little prince, and afterwards slay themselves; since, worn out by toil and confinement, they were utterly desperate. When this came to the ears of the cruel and ungodly queen, she rent her garments for grief, and cried aloud, "O Severinus, servant of the Lord, thus are the insults I have offered avenged by thy God! With profuse prayers thou hast called down vengeance upon my scorn, that thou might be avenged in my offspring!" So, running to and fro, with manifold contrition and pitiable lamentation, she acknowledged that she was smitten by this blow in recompense for the crime of scorn which she had committed against the servant of God. And she instantly dispatched horsemen to seek his pardon; and sent back the Romans whom that very day she had removed, and interceding for whom Severinus had been visited with her scorn. The goldsmiths received the surety of an oath, released the child, and were at the same time themselves released.

When he heard these things, the most reverent servant of Christ returned unbounded thanks to the Creator: who doth sometimes postpone answering prayer, in order that with the increase of faith, hope, and love he may grant greater blessings than are asked. For the omnipotence of the Saviour brought it to pass that when the cruel woman subjected the free to slavery, she was compelled to restore the slaves to liberty.

When these wonders had been accomplished, the queen forthwith hastened with her husband to the servant of God, and showed him her son, who, she acknowledged, had been rescued by his prayers from the brink of death. And she promised that she would never again resist his commands.

CHAPTER IX

NOT only was the servant of God endowed with the gift of prophecy, but also his diligence in redeeming captives was great. For he applied himself with eagerness to the task of restoring to their native liberty those oppressed by the sway of the barbarians.

Meanwhile he instructed a certain man, whom with wife and children he had redeemed, to cross the Danube, and seek out an unknown man at the weekly market of the barbarians. Divine revelation had shown him the man so clearly that he told even his stature and the color of his hair, his features, and the fashion of his clothing, and showed in what part of the market the messenger was to find him. He added that whatever the person, when found, should say to the messenger, the latter, returning in all haste, should report to him.

So the messenger departed, and to his astonishment found everything even as the man of God had foretold. He was amazed to find the man Severinus had described; who then questioned him, saying, " Thinkest thou that I can find someone to conduct me to the man of God, whose fame is everywhere spread abroad ? I will pay what price he wishes. For long have I importuned the holy martyrs, whose relics I bear, that sometime my unworthiness may be freed from this service, which hitherto I have maintained not out of rash presumption but by pious necessity." Then the messenger of the man of God made himself known to him. Severinus received with due honor the relics of Saint Gervasius and Saint Protasius the martyrs,[1] placed them in the church which he had built within the monastery, and committed them to

[1] There is an account of Gervasius and Protasius, the martyrs of Milan, in Tillemont's *Ecclesiastical Memoirs* (English translation by Thomas Deacon, London, 1731–35, ii, pp. 61–67).

the care of the priests. In that place he assembled the relics of vast numbers of martyrs; but he always acquired them on the strength of a previous revelation, for he knew that the adversary often creeps in [1] under the guise of sanctity.[2]

He was asked to accept the honorable office of bishop. But he closed the matter with a determined refusal. It was enough for him, he said, that, withdrawn from his beloved solitude, he had come by divine direction to that province to live among the pressing, crowding throngs. Nevertheless he wished to give a pattern to the monks, and urged them to follow earnestly in the steps of the sainted fathers, and thence to gain instruction in holy conduct. They must strive, he admonished them, that he who hath forsaken parents and the world look not back and desire the allurements of worldly display which he had sought to escape. On this point he referred to the

---

[1] Adopting Velserus's reading *subrepere*.

[2] Severinus was not the first to adopt this laudable attitude of caution in dealing with supposed relics. Sulpicius Severus, *De Beati Martini Vita*, 11, tells that Saint Martin, finding no clear evidence as to the contents of a tomb supposed to be hallowed by the remains of martyrs, prayed for a divine revelation. "Then he turned to the left, and saw close at hand a foul and savage ghost. He commanded the spectre to tell his name and desert. The spectre made known his name, he confessed his crime; he had been a robber, put to death for his wicked deeds, honored by the blunder of the mob; he had nothing in common with martyrs; they were in glory, he was in torment. The bystanders heard the spectre's voice, but did not see his form. Then Martin related what he had seen, and ordered that the altar which was there should be removed from the place. So he set free the people from the error of that superstition."

terrible example of Lot's wife.[1]   He admonished likewise that the incentives to lusts must be mortified in
the fear of the Lord; and declared that the fires of
sensual delights cannot be conquered, except through
the grace of God they be quenched in the fountain of
tears.

CHAPTER X

THERE was a janitor [2] at the monastery church, Maurus by name, whom Saint Severinus had redeemed
from the hands of the barbarians.   One day the man
of God warned him, saying, " Take heed to-day not
to go away anywhere: otherwise thou shalt be in
imminent peril."   But the janitor, contrary to the
warning of the great father, and persuaded by a lay-

[1] Genesis, xix, 26; Luke, xvii, 32.

[2] That this is here the meaning of *aedituus* is shown by the Table
of Chapters, where it is represented by *ostiarius*.   The office of *aedituus* in the pagan temple, however, corresponds rather to that of
custos in the Christian church (see Chapter I, above), being a position
of some dignity.   Ausonius, *Commemoratio Professorum Burdigalen-
sium*, x, 22–30, speaks of Phoebicius, a professor who had been *Beleni
aedituus*.   DuCange gives the definition " AEDITUUS, Ostiarius,
gradus ecclesiasticus; cui aedis sacrae custodia incumbit, *custos* ":
an impossible one, since *ostiarius* and *custos* are quite different officials.
The word never really became naturalized in Christian literature.
Paulinus of Nola uses it, it is true (*Epistolae*, i, 10; in Migne's *Patrologia Latina*, vol. lxi, col. 158); but he was a friend and correspondent
of Ausonius.

Theo Sommerlad, *Die Lebensbeschreibung Severins als kulturgeschichtliche Quelle* (Leipsic, 1903), p. 33, fails to notice that Eugippius
uses *aedituus* and *ostiarius* interchangeably both at this place and
in Chapter XVI, below, and accordingly wrongly considers *aedituus*
equivalent to the *ecclesiae custos* of Chapter I.

man, went out at midday to gather fruit [1] at the second milestone from Favianis.　Presently he and the layman were made captives by barbarians and carried across the Danube.　In that hour the man of God, reading in his cell, suddenly closed the book, and said, "Seek Maurus speedily!"　When the janitor was nowhere found, Severinus crossed the streams of the Danube in all haste, and hurried after the robbers, whom the people called Scamarae.[2]　Stricken with awe by his reverend presence, they humbly restored the captives whom they had taken.

CHAPTER XI

WHILE the upper towns of Riverside Noricum yet stood, and hardly a castle [3] escaped the attacks of the barbarians, the fame and reputation of Saint Severinus shone so brightly that the castles vied with each other

---

[1] The country along the Danube was probably then, as now, rich in orchards.　*Expositio totius Mundi et Gentium*, 57; A. A. Muchar, *Das römische Norikum* (Grätz, 1825–26), ii, p. 186.

[2] These organized bands of robbers appear again early in the sixth century, beyond the Danube (Jordanes, *De Rebus Geticis*, 58; Amédée Thierry, *Histoire d'Attila et de ses Successeurs*, Paris, 1856, i, pp. 288 f.); and, about 570, in Pannonia, under the name of Σκαμάρεις (Menander Protector, Bonnae, 1829, p. 313).

[3] *Castellum.*　Knoell considers that the word is equivalent to 'town' (*oppidum*).　But in Chapter XVII Eugippius contrasts the terms, saying 'towns or castles' (*oppida vel castella*).

Not forgetting that in the Vulgate *castellum* is the regular rendering for the Greek κώμη, 'village', I am inclined to think that the proper meaning in the Life is 'fortified town', or perhaps one might

in inviting his company and protection; believing that no misfortune would happen to them in his presence. This came to pass not without the aid of divine grace, that all might stand in awe of his commands, as of heavenly oracles, and be armed for good works through his example.

Moreover the holy man, summoned by the prayers of the vicinage, came to a castle named Cucullis,[1] and there a mighty miracle was wrought, which I cannot pass by in silence. We heard the amazing story from Marcianus, a citizen of the same town, later our priest. A part of the populace of Cucullis continued to practise abominable sacrifices at a certain spot.[2] When he learned of this sacrilege, the

---

say ' fort ' in the frontier sense of a fortified settlement. See Du Cange, *Glossarium Mediae et Infimae Latinitatis, s. v.;* and compare Salvian, *De Gubernatione Dei,* v, 44.

[1] Now Kuchel.

[2] Amédée Thierry interprets these as " sacrifices humains, pour apaiser la destinée." *Récits de l'Histoire Romaine au Vᵉ Siècle* (Paris, 1860), p. 148. It is doubtful if we are justified in pushing specification so far. Any heathen rites would have appeared ' abominable ' both to Severinus and to Eugippius. A Christian writer who wishes to accuse pagans of human sacrifices is likely to make the charge in so many words. Ennodius does so (*De Vita Beati Antoni,* 13) in speaking of the heathen barbarian tribes — Franks, Heruli, Saxons — who were ravaging the Pannonias at this time or a little later.

Mention was made above (Chapter V, note) of this passage in the Life of Antonius. Though Ennodius speaks of ' the Pannonias,' the connection makes it clear that his account is intended to apply also to Noricum, particularly the territory about Lauriacum. Antonius was nephew of Constantius, bishop of Lauriacum, who is named below (Chapter XXX), and after the death of Severinus remained at Lauriacum under the protection of his uncle until the latter's decease.

man of God addressed the people in many discourses.
He persuaded the priests of the place to enjoin a three
days' fast; and he instructed that waxen tapers
should be brought from each house, and that every-
one should fasten his taper with his own hand to the
wall of the church. Then, when the customary
psalm-singing was completed, and the hour of the
sacrifice arrived, the man of God exhorted the priests
and deacons that with all alacrity of heart they should
join him in prayer to their common Lord; that the
Lord might show the light of his knowledge to dis-
tinguish those guilty of sacrilege. So while he was
praying with them at great length, weeping much,
and on his knees, the greater part of the tapers, those
namely which the faithful had brought, were suddenly kindled by divine agency. The rest remained
unlighted, being the tapers of those who had been
polluted by the aforesaid sacrilege, but, wishing to
remain hidden, had denied it. Thus those who had
placed them were revealed by the divine test; and
straightway they cried out, and by their behavior
sufficiently betrayed the secrets of their hearts. Convicted by the witness of their tapers, and by open
confession, they bore witness to their own sacrilegious
acts.

O merciful power of the Creator, enkindling tapers
and souls! The fire was lighted in the tapers, and
shone with reflected light in the emotions! The
visible light melted into flames the substance of the
wax, but the invisible light dissolved the hearts of the

penitents into tears! Who would believe, that afterward those whom the error of sacrilege had ensnared were more distinguished for good works than those whose tapers had been divinely lighted ?

CHAPTER XII

AT another time, in the territory of the same castle, swarms of locusts had settled, consuming the crops, and destroying everything with their noxious bite.[1] Therefore, being smitten by this pest, the priests and the other inhabitants promptly betook themselves with urgent prayers to Saint Severinus, saying: " That this great and horrible plague may be removed, we ask the tried suffrage of thy prayers, which by the recent great miracle of the tapers lighted from heaven we have seen to avail much before the Lord." He answered them with great piety. " Have ye not read," he said, " what the divine authority commanded a sinful people through the prophet: ' Turn ye to me with all your heart, and with fasting, and with weeping,'[2] and a little after, ' sanctify a fast,' he saith,

[1] According to Marcellinus Comes, *Chronicon*, "numberless battalions of locusts wasted the harvest of Phrygia " in 456. Accounts of the devastations of these insects in 873 (throughout Europe) and in 1195 and 1242 (in the Austrian lands) may be found in Curschmann's *Hungersnöte im Mittelalter*, pp. 100 f., 157, 175. In 1242, if we may believe the chronicler, " Locusts of huge size invaded Austria in such numbers, that they consumed most of the vineyards and orchards, and moreover gnawed to pieces horses and cattle feeding in the fields."

[2] Joel, ii, 12.

'call a solemn assembly, gather the congregation,'[1]
and the rest which follows? Therefore fulfill by meet
works what ye teach, that ye may readily escape the
evil of the present time. Let no one go out to his field,
as if concerned to oppose the locusts by human effort;
lest the divine wrath be yet more provoked." Without delay all gathered together in the church, and each
in order sang psalms as was their custom. Every age
and sex, even such as could not form the words,
offered prayer to God in tears, alms were continually
given, whatever good works the present necessity
demanded were fulfilled, as the servant of God had
instructed.

While all were occupied with exertions of this sort,
a certain very poor man forsook the work of God that
was begun, to look after his own field of standing corn,
a little plot which stood among the sowings of the
others. And having gone out, and all day anxiously
and diligently driven away, so far as he could, the
threatening cloud of locusts, he then went to the
church to partake of the holy communion. But his
little patch of corn, surrounded by his neighbors'
many crops, was devoured by the dense swarm of
locusts.

The locusts were that night by divine command
removed from those territories: a proof of the great
power of faithful prayer. So when at dawn the viola-
tor and scorner of the holy work again went forth

---

[1] Joel, ii, 15, 16.

anxiously to his field, he found it swept perfectly bare
by the baleful work of the locusts, while all the sowings
round about were untouched. Utterly amazed, he
returned with doleful outcries to the castle. When he
· had published what had happened, all went out to see
the miracle; where the ravages of the locusts had
marked out as if by a ruled line the corn plot of this
contumacious fellow. Then he cast himself at their
feet and with lamentations begged for the pardon of his
sin by the aid of their intercession. Wherefore the
man of God took occasion to give a warning, and
taught all that they should learn to obey the Lord
omnipotent, whose commands even the locusts
observe.

But the poor man, weeping, declared that, for the
rest, he could obey the commands, if but a hope of
wherewithal he might live had been left him. Then
the man of God addressed the others. "It is just,"
he said, "that he who through his own punishment
hath given you an example of humility and obedience
should of your liberality receive sustenance for the
present year." So the poor man, both rebuked and
enriched by a collection from the faithful, learned
what loss unbelief inflicts, and what benefit God's
bounty bestows upon his worshippers.

CHAPTER XIII

NEAR a town called Juvao,[1] they went into the church one summer day to celebrate the evening service, but found no fire for lighting the lamps.   Unable to elicit a blaze in the usual way, by striking stones together, they were so long delayed in striking iron and stone [2] that the time of the evening service was passing.   But the man of God kneeled on the ground and prayed earnestly; and soon, in full view of three clerics who were present at the time, the taper which Saint Severinus held in his hand was lighted.[3]   By its light the sacrifice of eventide was completed in the custo-mary manner, and they returned thanks to God in all things.   Although he wished those who were present at this miracle to keep the fact secret, as in the case of

[1] Juvao or Juvavum, now Salzburg.

[2] " Rarissimus praeter exspectationem hic usus erat, si scriptorum auctoritas in hac re omnino quidquam valet."   M. H. Morgan, " De Ignis eliciendi Modis apud Antiquos," in *Harvard Studies in Classical Philology*, i (1890), p. 38.

[3] A similar miracle is related of Alveus, or Alneus, a Gallic saint of the sixth century.   " One night he arose for the early morning vigils, and entered the church with the rest of the brethren.   They found that the lights which usually burned there were out.   Saint Alveus kneeled in prayer.   The disciples searched for a light; but they could find no fire.   The hour was already late, and the disciples reminded the saint of the lateness of the hour.   Presently he rose from prayer, and made the sign of the cross above the waxen taper.   The taper was kindled instantly through the excellence of God and the merits of the saint, and gave a splendid light for all who were in the building." *Acta Sanctorum*, September, iii (1750), p. 808.

many mighty works which were performed through him by God's doing, yet the splendor of so great virtue could not be hid, but surpassingly kindled others to a great faith.

CHAPTER XIV

IT happened that a certain woman of Juvao was vexed by long continued sickness and lay half-dead, and the burial was already prepared. Her relatives, in mournful silence, repressed funereal lamentations at the voice of faith, and laid the sick woman's now almost lifeless body at the door of the saint's cell. When the man of God saw the entrance closed by the bed set against it, he said to them, " Why have ye done this ? " They answered, " That by thy prayer the dead may be restored to life." Then he said, bursting into tears, " Why do ye demand the great from the little ? I know myself utterly unworthy. O that I may deserve to find pardon for my sins! " They said, " We believe that if thou pray, she will live again." Then Saint Severinus straightway wept, and cast himself down in prayer; and when the woman forthwith arose, he addressed them: " Do not attribute to my works any of these things; for the vehemence of your faith hath merited this grace, and this cometh to pass in many places and nations, that it may be known that there is one God, who doeth wonders in heaven and on earth, calling forth the lost unto salvation, and bringing back the dead to life." The woman, her health restored, on the third day began to labor with her own hands in the fields, after the custom of the province.

CHAPTER XV

QUINTANIS [1] was a municipality of Raetia Secunda,[2] situated on the bank of the Danube. Near by on the other side ran a small river named Businca. Often the Businca, when swollen in time of flood by the overflow of the Danube, covered some spaces of the castle, because the latter stood on the plain. Moreover the inhabitants of this place had built outside the walls a wooden church which overhung the water, and was supported by posts driven into the riverbed and by forked props. In place of a flooring it had a slippery platform of boards, which were covered by the over-flowing water whenever it rose above the banks.

---

[1] In the *Notitia Dignitatum* Quintanis appears as a garrison town, commanded by the *praefectus alae primae Flavii Raetorum.* It is now represented by Osterhofen.

[2] Eugippius, whose earlier years were spent in the Danubian lands, tells of conditions there as he remembers them many years before the close of the fifth century. Raetia Secunda then included, nominally at least, the plain country between the Alps, the Inn, and the Danube; Raetia Prima, the whole central Alpine region. It seems clear that at the time of his writing (511) Raetia Secunda lay entirely in the Alps, and comprised the eastern part of the old Raetia Prima; while from the level country to the north, subject though it might be to the more or less shadowy overlordship of Theodoric the Ostrogoth as successor of Old Rome, all vestiges of the provincial name and administration had vanished. E. A. Quitzmann, *Die älteste Geschichte der Baiern* (Brunswick, 1873), p. 123.

Now through the faith of the people of Quintanis
Saint Severinus had been invited thither. Coming
at a time of drought, he asked why the boards were
seen bare and uncovered. The neighbors answered
that the frequent inundations of the river always
washed away anything that was spread on the boards.
But he said, "In Christ's name, let a pavement be
now laid upon the boards; from henceforth ye shall
see the river restrained by the command of heaven."
So when the pavement was finished, he went down
into a boat, took an axe, and, after offering prayer,
struck the posts; and, having cut the sign of the
venerable cross, said to the water of the river, "My
Lord Jesus Christ doth not permit thee to overpass
this sign of the cross." From that time, therefore,
when the river after its wont rose mountain high in
floods and encompassed the neighboring country as of
yore, it was lower than the site of the church, in such
wise that it never actually overpassed the sign of the
holy cross which the man of God had marked.

CHAPTER XVI

MOREOVER it happened that there died a highly
venerable priest of Quintanis, Silvinus by name. The
bier was placed in the church, and, according to the
custom, they passed the night watching and singing
psalms. When the dawn was already breaking, the
man of God asked all the weary priests and deacons

to go away for a little while, that after the toil of watching they might refresh themselves somewhat by sleep.
When they had gone out, the man of God asked the
doorkeeper, Maternus by name, whether all had
departed as he had bidden. When Maternus answered
that all had gone out, " Not so," he said, " but there is
a woman hiding here." Then the janitor of the
church explored the walls a second time, and assured
him that no one remained within them. But the
soldier of Christ, the Lord revealing it to him, said,
" Some one is lurking here." So the doorkeeper
searched more diligently for the third time, and found
that a certain consecrated virgin had concealed herself
in a very obscure place. Therefore the doorkeeper
reproved her: " Why didst thou think that thy presence could be hid when the servant of God was
here ? " She answered, " Love of piety persuaded
me to do it: for when I saw all driven out, I thought
within myself that the servant of Christ would invoke
the divine majesty, and raise up this dead man."
Then the virgin departed, and the man of God, bowing
in prayer together with a priest, a deacon, and two
janitors, prayed with many tears that the supernal
power might reveal a work of its wonted majesty.
Then, as the priest ended the prayer, the saint thus
addressed the corpse: " In the name of our Lord
Jesus Christ, holy priest Silvinus, speak with thy
brothers! " But when the dead man opened his eyes,
the man of God with difficulty persuaded those present
to restrain their joy and keep silent. And again he

speaketh unto him, " Shall we ask the Lord that he deign to grant thee still in this life to us, his servants ?" But he saith, " By the Lord I adjure thee, let me not be held here longer, and cheated of the everlasting rest in the possession of which I have seen myself." And immediately, when he had spoken, the dead man was at rest.[1]

Now this event was so concealed at the earnest request of Saint Severinus, that no one knew of it until after his death. Yet I learned what I have reported from the account of Marcus the subdeacon and Maternus the janitor. For the priest and the deacon, witnesses of this great miracle, are known to have died before the saint, to whom they had sworn to reveal to no one that which they had seen.

CHAPTER XVII

NOT only did the grace of Christ make Saint Severinus rich in such gifts, but also from his innate goodness he took so great care of captives and the needy that almost all the poor through all the towns and castles

---

[1] The gratitude of the catechumen recalled to life by Saint Martin was greater in proportion as his reception in the other world had been different. Sulpicius Severus, *De Beati Martini Vita*, vii, 4–6.

An engraving which represents this scene is mentioned in the Preface. There is another in J. H. von Falckenstein's *Antiquitates et Memorabilia Nordgaviae Veteris* (Schwabach, 1734–43), i, tab. vii, opposite p. 202. The latter is of especial interest in that it portrays the two doorkeepers, or janitors, in military costume, one of them leaning upon a huge battle-axe.

were fed by his activity. To these he ministered with such cheerful concern, that he believed himself to be filled or to abound in all good things only when he saw that the needy had their bodily wants supplied.

Though he himself was not in the least enfeebled by repeated week-long fasts, yet he felt himself afflicted by the hunger of the unfortunate. When they saw his pious largess to the poor, great numbers, although they were straitened with hunger under the harsh sway of the barbarians, faithfully gave the poor the tithes of their crops. Though this commandment is familiar to all from the law,[1] yet these observed it with

[1] Paul Viard, *Histoire de la Dîme Ecclésiastique* (Dijon, 1909), gives an excellent account of the origin of tithing in the early church, and also (pp. 44 f., 49) discusses this passage at length. Some of his conclusions may be briefly stated as follows. The only references to tithes in the Gospels (Matthew, xxiii, 23; Luke, xi, 42; xviii, 12) are in rebuke of the hypocrisy of the Pharisees. The Christians of the first four centuries did not recognize the Jewish tithe. They did in some instances acknowledge the tax of the first fruits. Insistence upon the tithe begins to appear about the end of the fourth century. In the East, its champion was Saint John Chrysostom (*In Matthaeum Homilia lxix (lxv)*, in Migne's *Patrologia Graeca*, lviii, col. 615). In the West, it was advocated in two forms. Jerome (*Explanatio in Malachiam*, iii, 7, in Migne's *Patrologia Latina*, xxv, coll. 1568–1571; and *Epistola ad Nepotianum de Vita Clericorum et Sacerdotum*, in Migne, xxii, col. 531) considers that the ancient law is still in force, and that the proceeds of the tithe should be for the support of the clergy. Augustine likewise (*Sermones*, lxxxv, 4, in Migne, xxxviii, col. 522) holds to the obligation of the tithe, at least upon the conscience, using the text Matthew, v, 20, " except your righteousness shall exceed the righteousness of the scribes and Pharisees "; but he directs it to the support of the poor. The later development of church polity, finally crystallized into definite enactments at the second council of Mâcon in 585, was a compromise between these two views. Severinus, on the

grateful devotion, as though they were hearing it given by the lips of an angel present among them. The cold, too, was felt by the man of God only in the nakedness of the poor. Indeed, he had received from God the special gift of remaining vigorous and active, hardened by his wonderful abstinence, in a land of bitter cold.

We spoke of tithes for the support of the poor. He was wont to send letters, urging the communities of Noricum [1] also to give them. This became their custom, and once, when they had sent to him a quantity of clothing to be distributed, he asked the attendants whether the town of Tiburnia [2] was sending a like contribution. They answered that men from that place also would soon arrive. But the man of God signified that they should not come, and foretold that the offering which they had delayed must be made to the barbarians. Accordingly, not long after the citizens of Tiburnia were beleaguered by the Goths, and fought them with varying fortune; and under the

other hand, follows Saint Augustine. " Probably," says M. Viard, " he did not speak of the tithe in the exact sense of the word; he wished merely to call forth the charitable gifts of the communities that he evangelized. It is very probable that the saint thought, in doing this, to revive the ancient tithe, modifying it, however, according to the needs of the moment and his personal disinterestedness. The biographer has exaggerated this thought of his hero in order to make it appear an actuality."

[1] Here, as elsewhere when he uses the word without a modifier, Eugippius means Noricum Mediterraneum, the interior or southern province, of which Tiburnia was the chief town.

[2] Teurnia in inscriptions. Now Sanct Peter im Holz, near Spital.

terms of peace, which they obtained with difficulty, they presented to the enemy, among other things, the largess, already collected, which they had delayed to send to the servant of God.[1]

CHAPTER XVIII

LIKEWISE the citizens of the town of Lauriacum,[2] in spite of many warning exhortations from Saint Severinus, had delayed offering to the poor the tithes of their crops. They were pinched with hunger, and the yellow of the ripening harvest showed that relief was at hand. But when a destructive rust unexpectedly appeared, and was on the point of damaging the crops, they immediately came and cast themselves down before Saint Severinus, and acknowledged the punishment of their stubbornness. But the soldier of

[1] The siege of Tiburnia may well be assigned to the year 473. See Chapter V, note. It is then probable that the surrender of the collection of clothing was an important, though hardly a decisive factor in restoring peace between the citizens and the ragged Goths; who, according to Jordanes (*De Rebus Geticis*, 56), entered upon the campaign because food and clothing were beginning to fail them. " Minuentibus se deinde hinc inde vicinarum gentium spoliis, coepit et Gothis victus vestituaque deesse: et hominibus, quibus dudum bella alimoniam praestitissent, pax coepit esse contraria; omnesque cum clamore magno ad regem Theodemir accedentes Gothi orant, quacumque parte vellet ductaret exercitum."

[2] The chief town of Riverside Noricum. Now Ens, or the small place Lorch, near Ens; authorities differ. At the time of the *Notitia Dignitatum* Lauriacum was defended by a strong garrison of soldiers, under the *praefectus legionis secundae*, and by a squadron of the Danube flotilla.

Christ comforted the feeble ones with spiritual words, saying, "Had ye offered tithes for the poor, not only would ye enjoy an everlasting reward, but ye would also be able to abound in present comforts. But since ye rebuke your sin by your own confession, I promise you, by the goodness of the Lord, that this mighty rust shall cause no damage whatever; only let not your faith waver any more." This promise rendered the citizens from that time on more ready to pay the tithes. Then, as was his wont, he urged that a fast be proclaimed. When this had ended, a gentle rain relieved from danger the harvest of which they had despaired.[1]

CHAPTER XIX

BATAVIS[2] is a town lying between two rivers, the Aenus and the Danube. There Saint Severinus had established after his wonted fashion a cell for a few monks, because he himself not infrequently came thither at the request of the citizens; particularly on

[1] Caesar Baronius supposes that this chapter and passages in Sidonius Apollinaris (*Epistolae*, vi, 12) and Gregory of Tours (*Historia Francorum*, ii, 24) relate to a general famine, which, he believes, afflicted the northern provinces in 475. "Quae Gallias vexavit dira fames, aeque afflixit Raetios, Noricos, et alios Boreales populos his finitimos." *Annales Ecclesiastici, a.* 475, sects. 30–35. There seems, however, no sufficient reason for linking the dearth at Lauriacum with that in Gaul, in the winter of 474–75, of which Sidonius and Gregory speak. The latter was caused, not by the fault of the season, but by the depredations of the Visigoths.

[2] Now Passau.

account of the constant incursions of the Alamanni, whose king, Gibuldus, greatly honored and loved him.

Now on a certain occasion Gibuldus came eagerly to see him. That the king might not encumber Batavis by his visit, the saint went out to meet him, and addressed the king with so great firmness, that Gibuldus began to tremble violently before him, and declared to his armies, as he withdrew, that never, in war or in any peril, had he been smitten with such trembling. And when he gave to the servant of God his choice, to give what command he would, the most pious teacher asked that the king should pay attention rather to his own best interests, restrain his nation from laying waste the Roman territory, and set free without ransom the captives his followers had made.

Then the king appointed that Severinus should direct some one from his own followers to bring this work more speedily to completion. Forthwith Deacon Amantius was dispatched, and followed in the king's path; but, though he watched before his gates many days, he could not secure an audience. As he was turning back, very sorrowful because his appointed task had not been accomplished, a man appeared in the form of Saint Severinus, who accosted him menacingly, and, as he stood in utter terror, bade him follow. As he followed in fear and excitement, he came to the king's door; and immediately the guide that had gone before him vanished from his wondering eyes. But the king's messenger asked the deacon whence he came and what he wished. He told his errand briefly, gave letters to the king, and received others from him, and returned home. He conveyed back about seventy captives, and moreover brought the pleasing promise of the king, that when he had diligently searched through the province, he would send back all the captives that were to be found there.

Later Saint Lucillus the priest was selected to attend to this matter, and recovered from captivity a great number of unfortunates.

CHAPTER XX

So long as the Roman dominion lasted, soldiers were maintained in many towns at the public expense to guard the boundary wall.[1] When this custom ceased, the squadrons of soldiers and the boundary wall were blotted out together. The troop at Batavis, however, held out.[2] Some soldiers of this troop had gone to Italy to fetch the final pay to their comrades, and no one knew that the barbarians had slain them on the way. One day, as Saint Severinus was reading in his cell, he suddenly closed the book and began to sigh greatly and to weep. He ordered the bystanders to

[1] Saint Augustine (*De Civitate Dei*, xviii, 18) tells of the corn, called *Retica annona*, sent from Italy for the supply of the soldiers in Raetia: " dicebat . . . narrasse quae passus est, caballum se scilicet factum annonam inter alia jumenta bajulasse militibus, quae dicitur Retica, quoniam ad Retias deportatur."

[2] The *cohors nova Batavorum*, according to the *Notitia Dignitatum*. The town, that is, was a military station, and took its name from the garrison.

run out with haste to the river, which he declared was in that hour besprinkled with human blood; and straightway word was brought that the bodies of the soldiers mentioned above had been brought to land by the current of the river.

CHAPTER XXI

ONE Paulinus, a priest, had come to Saint Severinus, whose fame was extending.[1] He tarried some days in the company of the saint. When he wished to return home, Severinus said to him, " Hasten, venerable priest; for, beloved, the episcopal dignity shall speedily adorn thee, even if, as we believe, thou opposest the desire of the peoples." And presently, when he returned to his own country, the word of the prophet was fulfilled unto him. For the citizens of Tiburnia, which is the metropolis of Noricum, compelled him to assume the preëminence of the highest priesthood.

[1] It would indeed be an evidence of an extensive fame, were we able to accept Mr. Hodgkin's ingenious conjecture as to the source of the penultimate name of the celebrated philosopher and poet Anicius Manlius Severinus Boethius, who was born at Rome probably during the eighth decade of the fifth century. *Italy and her Invaders*, iii (1885), p. 523 (or 2d ed., 1896, p. 471): " Severinus was no doubt given to him in honour of one of the holiest names of the fifth century, the saintly hermit of Noricum."

CHAPTER XXII

FOR a church beyond the walls of Batavis, in a place named Bojotro,[1] across the Aenus, where Severinus had built a cell for a few monks, relics of martyrs were sought. When the priests were accordingly pushing themselves forward that they might be sent to fetch relics,[2] Saint Severinus uttered this warning: " Though all wrought by mortals' toil passeth away, yet most swiftly must these buildings above others be abandoned." And he said that they ought to make no effort for relics of the saints, because the blessing of Saint John would be brought to them without their asking.

Meantime the citizens of Batavis approached the saint, and besought him to go to Feba, prince of the Rugii, to ask permission for them to trade. He said to them, " The time of this town is at hand, that it remain deserted like the rest of the upper castles and uninhabited. Why, then, is it necessary to provide merchandise for places where in future no merchant can appear ? " They replied that he ought not to

[1] Now Innstadt.

[2] *Sanctuaria*. *Reliquiae* is also used with the same meaning; as, for example, three lines above. The relics need not be of any great extent. Gregory the Great gave orders on at least three occasions that *sanctuaria* or *reliquiae* of Severinus himself should be furnished for the consecration of churches or oratories. *Epistolae*, iii, 19; ix, 181; xi, 19. This was a hundred years after the saint had been securely buried.

mock them, but to aid them with his wonted direction. A certain priest, filled with the spirit of Satan, added, " Go, saint, I beg, go quickly, that for a little space thy departure may give us rest from fastings and vigils." At this saying the man of God was oppressed with great weeping, because a priest, in public, had burst forth in ridiculous gabbling.   For open scurrility is a witness of hidden sins.   When the saint was asked by the brethren why he was weeping thus, " I see," he said, " a heavy blow that in my absence shall straightway befall this place; and, with groaning I must say it, the shrine of Christ shall so overflow with human blood, that even this place must be desecrated."   For he was speaking in the baptistery. Therefore he went down the Danube by ship a hundred miles and more to his old monastery, larger than the others, near the walls of Favianis.   As he was going down the river, Hunimund,[1] accompanied by a

---

[1] Probably Hunimund, king of the Suevi, whose raid into Dalmatia and hostilities with the Ostrogoths are described by Jordanes, *De Rebus Geticis*, 53–55.   Eduard von Wietersheim, indeed, in his *Geschichte der Völkerwanderung* (2d ed., Leipsic, 1880–81), ii, p. 324, expresses the belief that the coincidence in name is purely accidental. But if the Hunimund of Eugippius was not Hunimund the Suevian king, who was he ?   Eugippius through his whole work is perfectly definite in his identification of persons.   He names in all some fifty characters, aside from those mentioned in the Bible or in the church fathers.   Each is carefully labelled with the appropriate word or phrase, except two, Stilicho (Chapter XXXVI) and Hunimund.   It is a fair inference that Eugippius left these names unqualified — just as, for example, one would now in similar references that of Napoleon or of Blücher — because no label seemed needed, either for Stilicho, the great general of the Western Empire, or for Hunimund,

few barbarians, attacked the town of Batavis, as the saint had foretold, and, while almost all the inhabitants were occupied in the harvest, put to death forty men of the town who had remained for a guard. The priest who had spoken sacrilegious words in the baptistery against the servant of Christ fled for refuge to the same place, and was slain by the pursuing barbarians. For in vain did the offender against God and enemy of truth seek protection in the place where he had so impudently transgressed.

CHAPTER XXIII

ONCE while Saint Severinus was reading the Gospel in the monastery at Favianis, after offering prayer he arose, ordered a skiff to be instantly prepared for him, and said to the astonished bystanders, "Blessed be the name of the Lord; we must go to meet the relics of the sainted martyrs." They crossed the Danube without delay, and found a man sitting on the farther bank of the river, who besought them with many prayers to conduct him to the servant of God, whose fame was widespread, and to whom he had long wished to come. The servant of Christ was pointed out to

king of the Suevi, a principal leader in a war, not yet remote in time, that had devastated Central Europe for years.

We may infer from the smallness of the force under the command of Hunimund that the attack on Bojotro was made after the destructive overthrow of the Suevi by the Ostrogoths; perhaps in 474 or 475. The sequence of Eugippius's narrative points to the same date.

him; and immediately and as a suppliant he offered him the relics of Saint John the Baptist, which he had kept by him for a long time. The servant of God received the relics with the veneration they deserved; and so the blessing of Saint John was bestowed unasked upon the church, as he had foretold, and Severinus consecrated the relics by the hands of the priests.

CHAPTER XXIV

THERE was a town called Joviaco,[1] twenty miles and more distant from Batavis. Thither the man of God, impressed as usual by a revelation, sent a singer of the church, Moderatus by name; admonishing that all the inhabitants should quit that place without delay. For imminent destruction threatened them if they despised his commands.[2] Some were in doubt over so great a presage, while others did not believe it at all. Therefore yet again he sent one unto them, a certain

[1] Schlögen.

[2] F. W. Rettberg believes that Severinus may have owed his foreknowledge of barbarian raids to secret information received from his friends among the Germans. *Kirchengeschichte Deutschlands*, i, pp. 232 f. This view is held also by Felix Dahn. *Gelehrte Anzeigen* (Munich), 21 Sept. 1859, coll. 270 f. Reinhold Pallmann declines to accept it. *Die Geschichte der Völkerwanderung* (Gotha, etc., 1863–64), ii, p. 400, n. 1.

George Thomas Stokes remarks that Severinus " seems to have been gifted with some kind of second-sight, similar to that which Adamnan's Life of St. Columba claims for the Celtic saint of the following century." Smith and Wace's *Dictionary of Christian Biography*, iv (London, 1887), p. 627.

man of Quintanis, to whom he said, weeping, "Make
haste! Declare unto them that if they stay there this
night, they shall without delay be made captives!"
He bade that Saint Maximianus too, a priest of
spiritual life, should be urgently warned; that he at
least, leaving the scorners behind, through the compassion of heaven might escape. The servant of God
said that he was in great sorrow over him, lest haply
he might postpone obedience to the saving command,
and so be exposed to the threatening destruction.
Accordingly the messenger of the man of God went
and fulfilled his orders; and when the others in their
unbelief hesitated, he did not tarry a moment, though
the priest strove to keep him and wished to extend to
him the courtesy of his hospitality. That night the
Heruli made a sudden, unexpected onslaught, sacked
the town, and led most of the people into captivity.
They hanged the priest Maximianus on a cross. When
the news came, the servant of God grieved sorely that
his warnings had been disregarded.

CHAPTER XXV

LATER a man from Noricum, Maximus by name, came
to visit the servant of God, as was his frequent custom.
Pursuant to their established friendship, he tarried
some days in the monastery of the saint. Then
Severinus informed him by his oracles that his country was about to experience a sudden and heavy
disaster. Maximus took a letter addressed to Saint

Paulinus the bishop, and in all haste returned home.
Accordingly Paulinus, prepared by the contents of the
letter, wrote to all the castles of his diocese, and
strongly admonished them to meet the coming mis-
chief and disaster by a three days' fast, as the letter of
the man of God had indicated. They obeyed these
commands, and the fast was ended, when lo, a vast
multitude of the Alamanni, minions of Death, laid
everything waste. But the castles felt no danger.
The trusty cuirass of fasting, and praiseworthy humility of heart, with the aid of the prophet, had armed
them boldly against the fierceness of the enemy.

CHAPTER XXVI

LATER, a leper from the territory of Milan came to
Saint Severinus, attracted by his fame. When he
prayed and begged to be made whole, Severinus
decreed a fast, and commended the leper to his
monks; and through the work of God's grace he was
forthwith cleansed. When he had been made whole
and was advised to return to his country, he threw
himself at the feet of the saint, imploring that he be
not compelled to go home again; desiring that he
might escape from the leprosy of sin as he had from
that of the flesh, and might close his life in the same
place with a praiseworthy end. The man of God
greatly admired his pious purpose, and with fatherly
command instructed a few monks to practise frequent

fasts with him and to continue in uninterrupted prayer, in order that the Lord might grant to him those things which were meet. Fortified by so great remedies, within the space of two months the man was freed from the fetters of mortal life.

CHAPTER XXVII

AT the same time the inhabitants of the town of Quintanis, exhausted by the incessant incursions of the Alamanni, left their own abodes and removed to the town of Batavis. But their place of refuge did not remain hidden from the Alamanni: wherefore the barbarians were the more inflamed, believing that they might pillage the peoples of two towns in one attack. But Saint Severinus applied himself vigorously to prayer, and encouraged the Romans in manifold ways by examples of salvation. He foretold that the present foes should indeed by God's aid be overcome; but that after the victory those who despised his admonitions should perish. Therefore the Romans in a body, strengthened by the prediction of the saint, and in the hope of the promised victory, drew up against the Alamanni in order of battle, fortified less with material arms than by the prayers of the saint. The Alamanni were overthrown in the conflict and fled. The man of God addressed the victors as follows. " Children, do not attribute the glory of the

present conflict to your own strength.[1]　Know that
ye are now set free through the protection of God to
the end that ye may depart hence within a little space
of time, granted you as a kind of armistice.　So
gather together and go down with me to the town of
Lauriacum."　The man of God impressed these
things upon them from the fullness of his piety.　But
when the people of Batavis hesitated to leave their
native soil, he added, "Although that town also,
whither we go, must be abandoned as speedily as
possible before the inrushing barbarism, yet let us now
in like manner depart from this place."

As he impressed such things upon their minds, most
of the people followed him.　A few indeed proved
stubborn, nor did the scorners escape the hostile
sword.　For that same week the Thuringi stormed
the town; and of those who notwithstanding the
prohibition of the man of God remained there, a part
were butchered, the rest led off into captivity and made
to pay the penalty for their scorn.[2]

---

[1] With the view of Severinus may be contrasted that of Saint
Ambrose, *Epistolae*, xviii, 30: "deam esse victoriam crediderunt
[pagani], quae utique munus est, non potestas: donatur, non domina-
tur, legionum gratia, non religionum potentia"; "they have believed Victory to be a goddess, which is in truth a gift, not a power;
is bestowed, and does not rule; comes by the aid of legions, not by the
power of religion."

[2] There is some measure of justice in the comment which Pallmann
makes upon the conduct of Severinus in this instance.　"With his
words of discouragement Severinus divided the strength of the citizens.　Through his disheartening view of things, he brought a part
of them to despair, without helping in the least the others who did not

CHAPTER XXVIII

AFTER the destruction of the towns on the upper course of the Danube, all the people who had obeyed the warnings of Saint Severinus removed into the town of Lauriacum. He warned them with incessant exhortations not to put trust in their own strength, but to apply themselves to prayers and fastings and almsgivings, and to be defended rather by the weapons of the spirit.

Moreover one day the man of God appointed that all the poor be gathered together in one church, that he might, as custom demanded, dispense oil to them: a commodity which in those places was brought to market only after a most difficult transport by traders. Accordingly a great throng of the needy assembled, as if for the sake of receiving the benediction. No doubt the presence of this fluid, a costly food, swelled

join him; rather, weakening them. So was the strength of the brave citizens of Passau paralyzed." *Die Geschichte der Völkerwanderung,* ii, p. 397. It would not, however, be fair to make this citation from Pallmann without quoting also the passage (*ibid.*, pp. 400 f.) in which he sums up his opinion of the saint and his public activities. "It is a strange, noble, powerful figure, this monk. . . . A political head would certainly have acted wholly otherwise than Severinus. We do not know whether he would have had better success. Yet it was a piece of good fortune, that in the disastrous time after the death of Aëtius, when on every side the dissolution of the Empire, like the death of a human body, was beginning at the extremities, and the provinces one by one were renouncing their connection with Italy; when we see Gaul independent under Aegidius, Dalmatia under Marcellinus; that in Noricum, if no general arose, yet at least a pure and lofty spirit sought to do the works of righteousness."

the throng and the number of applicants. When the saint had finished the prayer, and made the sign of the cross, he uttered as usual, while all listened, the word of Holy Writ, "Blessed be the name of the Lord." Then he began with his own hand to fill the measures of oil for the attendants who conveyed it, copying as a faithful servant his Lord, who came not to be ministered unto, but to minister.[1] And, following in the way of the Saviour, he rejoiced that the substance was increased, which he poured out with his right hand, his left hand knowing not.[2] When the oil-vessels of the poor were filled, the oil in the hands of the attendants was not diminished. Now while the bystanders silently wondered at so great a blessing of God, one of them, whose name was Pientissimus, in amazement and great fear cried out, "My Lord! This pot of oil increases, and overflows like a fountain!" So, its miraculous powers having been betrayed, the welcome fluid was withdrawn. Straightway the servant of Christ cried out and said, "Brother, what hast thou done? Thou hast hindered the advantage of many: may the Lord Jesus Christ pardon thee!" So once the widow woman burdened with debts was bidden by Elisha the prophet from the small quantity of oil which she had to fill vessels not a few. After she had done this, and asked for yet more vessels from her sons, when she heard that there was not a vessel more, straightway the oil stayed.[3]

[1] Mark, x, 45.   [2] Matthew, vi, 3.   [3] II Kings, iv, 2–7.

CHAPTER XXIX

AT the same time Maximus of Noricum, of whom we have made mention above, kindled by the warmth of his faith, at midwinter, when the roads of that region are closed by the numbing cold, hastened to come to Saint Severinus. It was an enterprise of rash temerity, or rather, as was afterwards manifest, of fearless devotion. He had hired many companions, to carry on their backs, for the benefit of the captives and the poor, a collection of clothing which the people of Noricum had piously given.[1] So they set out, and attained the highest peaks of the Alps, where all night long the snow fell so thickly that it shut them in beneath the protecting shelter of a great tree, as a huge pit would inclose those who had fallen into it. And when they despaired utterly of their lives, since no aid (as they thought) was at hand, the leader of the companions saw in his sleep a vision of the man of God standing and saying unto him, "Fear not; complete your journey." They were instantly heartened by this revelation, and resumed their course, trusting in God rather than in the strength of their limbs; when suddenly by divine command a bear of monstrous size appeared at their side to show the way:[2] though in

---

[1] At an earlier date Noricum was celebrated for its export trade in clothing. *Expositio totius Mundi et Gentium*, 57.

[2] The friendliness to the righteous of beasts usually wild and savage is a common feature in early Christian narratives. See the index to Heribert Rosweyde's *Vitae Patrum* (2d ed., Antverpiae, 1628). There are instances of lions serving as guides in Rosweyde, pp. 231 a, 816 a; and of a wild ass in the same capacity, p. 229 a.

the winter time he usually hid in caves. He immediately disclosed the desired road, and for about two hundred miles, turning aside neither to the left nor to the right, showed a passable way. For he went just far enough ahead of them so that his fresh track broke out a path. So, leading through the desert wilderness, the beast did not forsake the men who were bringing relief to the needy, but with the utmost possible friendliness conducted them as far as human habitations. Then, having fulfilled his duty, he turned aside and departed: showing by the great service of his guidance what men ought to do for men, and how much love they ought to display, since here a savage beast showed the road to the despairing.

When the arrivals were announced to the servant of God, he said, " Blessed be the name of the Lord ! Let them enter, to whom a bear hath opened a way for their coming." When they heard this they marvelled with exceeding great amazement that the man of God should tell that which had happened in his absence.

CHAPTER XXX

THE citizens of the town of Lauriacum and the fugitives from the upper castles appointed scouts to explore the suspected places, and guarded against the enemy, so far as by human care they could. The servant of God, instructed by divine inspiration, arranged beforehand with prophetic mind that they should bring inside the city wall all their meagre property, in order that the foemen in their deadly foray, meeting with no human life, might be promptly forced by hunger to abandon their frightful and cruel designs. This he earnestly entreated for four days. When the fourth day already verged toward evening, he sent a monk, Valens by name, to Saint Constantius, bishop of the town,[1] and said to the others who remained, " Set the customary guards at the walls tonight, and keep a stricter watch; and beware of a sudden and treacherous assault by the foe." They declared to him that the scouts saw absolutely nothing of the enemy. But the servant of Christ did not cease to forewarn the hesitant, and cried out with a loud voice, affirming that they would be taken captive that same night unless they faithfully obeyed his commands. He often repeated the words, " If I shall be proved a liar, stone me." So at last they were compelled to guard the walls.

At the beginning of the night they sang psalms, as they were wont, and afterwards the men gathered in great numbers and commenced their watch. Then a nearby haystack, accidentally fired by a porter's torch, illuminated, but did not burn the city. When this happened, every one howled and shouted, and the enemy concealed in the woods and forests were terri-

[1] The best life of Constantius is by Marcus Hansitz (*Germania Sacra*, i, pp. 82–87). Hansitz believes that much of the success of Severinus in his work must have been due to the coöperation of Constantius.

The ' archbishopric of Lauriacum ' is a mediaeval forgery, long since wholly discredited.

fied by the sudden brightness and the shouting, and, thinking themselves detected, remained quiet. Next morning they surrounded the city, and ran to and fro everywhere; but when they found no food, they seized the herd of cattle of a certain man who in the face of the prophecies of the servant of God had stubbornly scorned to secure his possessions, and withdrew.

Now when they were gone the citizens sallied forth from the gates, and found ladders lying not far from the walls. These the barbarians had made ready for the destruction of the city, and had thrown away when they were disturbed in the night by the shouting. Therefore the citizens of Lauriacum humbly besought pardon from the servant of Christ, confessing that their hearts were harder than stones. They recognized from these events that the loveliness of prophecy bloomed in the saint. Assuredly the disobedient populace would all have gone into captivity, had not the accustomed prayer of the man of God kept them free; for as James the apostle bears witness, " The continual prayer of a righteous man availeth much." [1]

CHAPTER XXXI

FELETHEUS, sometimes called Feva, king of the Rugii, hearing that from all the towns by the advice of the servant of God the remnants that had escaped the barbarian sword had gathered at Lauriacum, took an

[1] James, v, 16.

army and came, purposing to bring them quickly into
his own power and to lead them away and settle them
in the towns, of which Favianis was one, that were
tributary to him and near him, and were separated
from the Rugii only by the Danube. Wherefore all
were deeply disturbed, and with prayers went to Saint
Severinus, that he might go forth to meet the king and
moderate his purpose. All night Severinus hastened,
and in the morning met him at the twentieth milestone
from the city. The king, much alarmed by his arrival,
averred that he was vastly distressed by the saint's
fatiguing journey, and inquired the causes of his
sudden visit. To whom thus answered the servant of
God: "Peace be unto thee, most excellent king. I
come to thee as ambassador of Christ, to beg compassion for the conquered. Reflect upon the grace, recall
to mind the divine favors, of whose repeated aid thy
father was sensible. Throughout the whole time of
his reign he never ventured to take any step without
my advice. He did not withstand my salutary
admonitions; and from frequent successes he learned
to recognize the great value of an obedient mind, and
how greatly it profiteth victors not to be puffed up by
their triumphs." And the king saith, "I will not
suffer this people, for whom thou comest as a friendly
intercessor, to be ruined by the cruel plundering of the
Alamanni and Thuringi, or slaughtered by the sword,
or reduced to slavery, when I have neighboring and
tributary towns in which they ought to be established." The servant of Christ firmly answered him

as follows: "Was it thy bow or sword that delivered these men from the continual ravages of robbers? Were they not rather reserved by the favor of God, that they might be able for a short while to obey thee? Therefore, most excellent king, do not now reject my counsel. Commit these subjects to my guardian care, lest by the constraint of so great an army they be ruined rather than removed. For I trust in my Lord, that he, who hath made me a witness of their calamities, shall make me a suitable leader to conduct them to safety."

The king was appeased by these moderate representations, and forthwith went back with his army. Therefore the Romans whom Saint Severinus had received in his guardian care left Lauriacum, were amicably established in the towns, and lived in friendly alliance with the Rugii.[1] But Severinus dwelt at Favianis in his old monastery, and ceased not to admonish the peoples and to foretell the future, declaring that all were to remove into a Roman province without any loss of liberty.

CHAPTER XXXII

AT about the same time King Odoacer addressed a friendly letter to Saint Severinus, and, mindful of that prophecy, by which of yore he had foretold that

[1] That this exodus was a partial one only, is indicated both by the laws of probability and by Ennodius's Life of Antonius, 10-14. Antonius remained under the protection of his uncle, Constantius, bishop of Lauriacum, for some time after the death of Severinus.

he should become king, entreated him to choose whatsoever gift he might desire.   In response to this august
invitation, the saint asked that one Ambrose, who was
living in exile, be pardoned.   Odoacer joyfully obeyed
his command.

Also, once when in the saint's presence many nobles
were praising Odoacer with the adulation usual among
men, Severinus asked on what king they were confer-
ring such great commendations.   They replied,
" Odoacer." " Odoacer," he said, " safe between thir-
teen and fourteen "; meaning of course the years of
his unchallenged sovereignty: and he added that they
should live to see the speedy fulfillment of his prophecy.

CHAPTER XXXIII

AT the entreaty of the townspeople, among whom he
had first won fame, Saint Severinus came to Comagenis.   One of the nobles of King Feletheus had a son,
a youth, who was wasted away by inveterate sickness
and for whose burial preparations were already in
progress.   When the nobleman learned that Severinus
was at Comagenis, he crossed the Danube and cast
himself at his feet.   Weeping, he said, " I believe, man
of God, that thy entreaty can procure from heaven a
swift recovery for my son."   Then Severinus offered
prayer.   The boy, who had been brought to him half-
dead, straightway arose whole, to the amazement of
his father, and forthwith returned home in perfect
health.

CHAPTER XXXIV

Likewise a certain leper, Tejo by name, attracted by the virtues of Saint Severinus, came from a far country, asking to be cleansed through his prayer. So he was given the customary command, and bidden ceaselessly and with tears to implore God, the giver of all grace. Why say more ? Through the prayers of the saint the leper was cleansed by the divine aid; as he altered his character for the better, he gained a change of color also; and he, and many others who knew of him, proclaimed far and wide the mighty works of the Eternal King.

CHAPTER XXXV

Bonosus, by birth a barbarian, was a monk of Saint Severinus, and hung upon his words. He was much afflicted by weakness of the eyes, and desired that cure be afforded him through the prayers of the saint. He bore it ill that strangers and foreigners experienced the aid of healing grace, while no cure or help was tendered to him. The servant of God said unto him, " Son, it is not expedient for thee to have clear sight in the bodily eyes, and to prefer distinct vision by the eye of the flesh. Pray rather that thy inner sight may be quickened." Bonosus was instructed by these admonitions, and was eager to see with the heart rather than with the flesh. He gained a wonderful power of unwavering continuance in prayer. After he had remained steadfastly for about forty years in the service of the monastery, he passed away in the same ardent faith in which he was converted.

CHAPTER XXXVI [1]

IN Bojotro, a place mentioned above, the humble teacher perceived that three monks of his monastery were stained with horrid pride. When he had ascertained that each of them upon being visited with reproach was hardened in his sin, he prayed that the Lord should receive them into the adoption of sons, and deign to reprove them with the paternal lash. Before he had ended his tearful prayer, the three monks were in one and the same instant seized violently by the devil and tormented, and with cries confessed the stubbornness of their hearts.

Let it not seem to any one cruel or wrong, that men of this sort are delivered " unto Satan for the destruction of the flesh," as the blessed apostle teacheth, " that the spirit may be saved in the day of the Lord Jesus." [2] For Saint Ambrose, bishop of Milan, said that the slave of Stilicho, who was found to be the

---

[1] This chapter is apparently out of the regular chronological sequence. Chapter XXVIII presupposes the abandonment or destruction of all the towns on the Danube above Lauriacum, including Bojotro. It is, however, the opinion of Pallmann (*Geschichte der Völkerwanderung*, ii, pp. 393 f.) and of Julius Jung (*Römer und Romanen in den Donauländern*, Innsbruck, 1877, p. 214) that there really was no break of the sort indicated by Eugippius in the continuity of occupation.

[2] I Corinthians, v, 5.

author of forged letters, ought to be delivered unto
Satan, that he might not dare to commit such crimes
in the future; and at the same moment, while the
word was yet in the bishop's mouth, the unclean spirit
seized the slave and began to rend him.[1] Sulpicius
Severus, too, relates,[2] on the authority of Postumianus,
that a certain man, admirable for his great virtues and
miracles, aiming to drive out from his heart the vanity
of ostentation into which he had fallen, procured by
entreaty " that power over him might be given the
devil for five months, and he be made like those whom
he himself had healed." And Sulpicius says, a little
further on, that accordingly " he was seized by the
devil, held in chains, and endured everything which
those possessed by devils are wont to suffer; until,
finally, in the fifth month he was cured, not merely
from the devil, but (what he needed and desired more)
from the fault."

So the man of God turned over the three monks to
the brethren, and subjected them for forty days to the
bitter remedy of fasting. When the days were fulfilled, he spake a prayer over them, and plucked them
forth from the power of the devil, and bestowed upon
them soundness not only of body but of mind. As a
result of this event, the saint was held in enhanced
awe and terror, and a greater fear of discipline possessed the rest.[3]

---

[1] Paulinus Mediolanensis, *Vita Ambrosii*, 43.

[2] *Dialogi*, i, 20, 7.

[3] We shall not be far astray if we suppose that the ' horrid pride '

CHAPTER XXXVII

MARCIANUS the monk, who was afterward priest, and who preceded me in the headship of the monastery, was sent by Severinus to Noricum in company with Brother Renatus. As the third day was passing, the saint said to the brethren, " Pray, dearly beloved, for at this hour grievous tribulation is upon Marcianus and Renatus, from which nevertheless they shall be freed by Christ's aid." Then the monks straightway wrote down what he had said; and when many months later Marcianus and Renatus returned, and made known the day and hour of their peril, at which they had escaped the barbarians, these were found to be just as had been written down.

of which the three monks were guilty was some form of insubordination. The relation between humility and obedience in the monk is discussed by H. B. Workman in his essay, *The Evolution of the Monastic Ideal* (London, 1913), pp. 68–74. " The third fundamental idea of Monasticism," he says, " first specifically introduced by Pachomius, was the renunciation of the will. This is sometimes called obedience, sometimes humility; in reality, from the Monastic standpoint the two tend to become one. The two are related as cause and effect; they are different aspects of that complete self-renunciation which is higher than any mere outer surrender. The man who has nailed his inner self to the cross cannot be otherwise than humble; while the humble man will show his humility by a perfect obedience."

CHAPTER XXXVIII

Also most blessed Severinus suddenly commanded one of the brethren, by name Ursus, to meet in advance a coming calamity by a strict fast of forty days, with abstinence from food, and lamentations, saying, "A bodily peril threatens thee, which through God's protection thou shalt avert by the remedy of a scanty diet of bread and water." So on the fortieth day a deadly pustule appeared on the arm of the fasting man, which he immediately showed to Severinus, approaching him as a suppliant. The holy servant of God said unto him, "Do not fear the crisis which was foretold thee forty days ago"; and straightway with his own hand made the sign of the cross over it; whereupon the fatal pustule vanished, to the amazement of the bystanders.

Let it suffice to have told of this one of his cures in his own household, that I may avoid the tediousness of a lengthy task. For often through the revelation of Christ he foretold the illnesses of his monks, and healed them through the same gifts by which he foresaw them.

CHAPTER XXXIX

The spiritual teacher, continuing instant in prayer and fasting, dwelt not far from the cell of his disciples. With them he regularly completed the morning prayers, and the proper psalm-singing in the evening.

The remaining times of prayer he fulfilled in the little oratory in which he lived. In his seasons of prayer he was often strengthened by celestial oracles, and through the grace of God foretold many things that were to come. He knew the secrets of many things, and, when there was need, made them known, and provided remedies for each patient, according as the kind of sickness demanded. His bed was a single mohair rug on the floor of the oratory.[1] Always, even while he slept, he wore the same garment.[2] He never broke his fast before sunset except on an appointed festival.[3] In Lent he was satisfied with one meal a

[1] The couch of Saint Anthony, the great Egyptian monk, was likewise a mohair rug; to which, in his case, a rush mat was added. Athanasius, *Vita Beati Antonii Abbatis* (Evagrius's translation), p. 38 a Rosweyde.

[2] Palladius (*Heraclidis Paradisus*, 35) tells a like story in praise of the Egyptian monk Paphnutius Cephala: "De quo tale refertur praeconium, quod per octoginta annos numquam habuerit duas simul tunicas."

[3] Eusebius (*Ecclesiastica Historia*, ii, 17; Crusé's translation, London, 1851, pp. 56 f., corrected) quotes Philo Judaeus, *De Vita Contemplativa*, in regard to the asceticism of the Therapeutae of Egypt. "None of them" (he says) "takes food or drink before the setting of the sun, since they judge that the search for wisdom should be prosecuted in the light, while it is appropriate that the necessities of the body should be attended to in the dark. Whence they assign to the one the day, and to the other a small portion of the night. But some of them do not remember their food for three days, when influenced by an uncommon desire for knowledge. And some are so delighted, and feast so luxuriously on the doctrines so richly and profusely furnished by wisdom, that they forbear even twice this time, and are scarcely induced to take necessary food even for six days." Eusebius considers that under the name of Therapeutae Philo describes the early Christians. Valesius (notes to *Eusebii Ecclesiastica*

week, yet his countenance shone with the same cheerfulness. He wept over the sins of others as if they were his own, and helped to overcome them by such aid as he could give.

CHAPTER XL

At last, after many struggles and long contests, Saint Severinus, through the revelation of God, perceived that he was about to pass from this world. He bade Feva, king of the Rugii, mentioned above, to come to him with his cruel wife Giso. He exhorted Feva, with salutary words, that in dealing with his subjects he should constantly bear in mind that he must render account to the Lord for the condition of his kingdom; and fearlessly added other admonitions. Then he stretched forth his hand, pointing to the king's breast, and reproachfully asked the queen, " Giso, which lovest thou the more, this soul, or gold and silver ? " And when she answered that she prized her husband above all riches, the man of God in his wisdom continued, " Therefore cease to oppress the innocent, lest their affliction result in the destruc-

Historia, edition of 1672, p. 34) believes the contrary. The matter is yet under discussion. H. B. Workman, *The Evolution of the Monastic Ideal*, p. 90, especially note 1.

The association of eating by night with asceticism appears to have survived, in a singularly altered form, in the religious body organized by George Rapp in Würtemberg on the model of the primitive church, and later established at Harmony, Pennsylvania. See *The Atlantic Monthly*, May, 1866, p. 535.

tion of your power. For thou often bringest to naught the clemency of the king." But she answered, " Why dost thou receive us so, servant of God ? " He replied, " I adjure you, I the lowly, who shall shortly stand in the presence of God, that ye restrain yourselves from unjust deeds, and apply yourselves to works of piety. Hitherto by God's help your kingdom hath been prospered. Henceforth look to it." The king and queen, much instructed by these admonitions, bade him farewell, and went away.[1]

Then the saint ceased not to address his people in the sweetness of love concerning the nearness of his departure. Indeed, he had done so ceaselessly before. " Know ye, brethren," he said, " that as the children of Israel were delivered out of the land of Egypt, so all the peoples of this land are destined to be freed from the unrighteous sway of the barbarians. For all shall depart from these towns with their possessions,

[1] The learned Bavarian historian, Johann Adlzreitter, floridly enlarges this conversation to three times its length in Eugippius, and makes it the most prominent feature in his long and curious summary of the Life. *Annalium Boicae Gentis Partes III* (1710), coll. 124 f.

The comment of A. F. Ozanam upon this interview, though quoted with approval by Montalembert (*Les Moines d'Occident*, i, p. 261) and Charles Kingsley (*The Hermits*, p. 238), is more rhetorically effective than just. " The history of invasions has many a pathetic scene: but I know none more instructive than the dying agony of that old Roman expiring between two barbarians, and less touched with the ruin of the empire than with the peril of their souls." *La Civilisation Chrétienne chez les Francs* (3d ed., Paris, 1861), pp. 41 f. It requires a certain amount of naïveté not to see that the saint's prime concern in his warnings is rather the tranquillity of the provincials than the souls' welfare of the royal couple.

and shall reach the Roman province without any loss by capture. But remember the command of the holy patriarch Joseph, in the words of whose testimony I, though unworthy and most lowly, make my request to you: 'God will surely visit you; and ye shall carry up my bones from hence.'[1] This shall profit, not me, but you. For these places, now thronged with inhabitants, shall be rendered a solitude so utterly waste that the enemy, thinking to find gold, shall dig up even the graves of the dead." The present issue in fact has proved the truth of his prophecy. But the most holy father, with pious forethought, ordered his body to be removed as a token; in order that when the general transmigration of the people should take place, the company of brethren which he had gathered might depart undivided, and, held together by the common bond of his memory, might endure as one holy society.

CHAPTER XLI

MOREOVER most blessed Severinus revealed two years or more in advance the day on which he was to pass from the body.[2] This he did in the following manner.

---

[1] Genesis, l, 25.

[2] Instances where saints are said to have predicted the day or even the hour of their decease are not rare in the mediaeval narratives; but, as compared with the present account, they are usually vague and perfunctory. A casual examination of a volume of the *Acta Sanctorum* taken at random — September, iii — reveals three cases, on pages 58, 293, and 806.

On the day of Epiphany, when Saint Lucillus the priest had announced in agitation that on the morrow he was to perform the annual rites of commemoration for the burial day of his abbot, Saint Valentine,[1] formerly bishop of the Raetias, the servant of God replied, " If Saint Valentine hath committed these rites to thee to be performed, I too, being about to depart from the body, bequeath to thee the care of my funeral festival, which shall be observed upon the same day." Lucillus, an old and broken man, was greatly shaken at this saying, and rather commended himself earnestly to the protection of Severinus, on the ground that he was likely to pass away first. But Severinus answered, " Holy priest, this thing which thou hast heard shall come to pass, nor shall the Lord's ordinance be brought to naught by the will of man."

[1] There is a life of Valentine in Matthaeus Rader's *Bavaria Sancta* (Monaci, 1615-27), i, ff. 24b, 25, 26a, with a fine engraving representing the saint in his arboreal retreat.

> " Rura Valentinum tutantur, et oppida pellunt.
> Fas regnat ruri, regnat in urbe nefas."

Valentine is also mentioned by Venantius Fortunatus (*Vita Sancti Martini*, iv, 644-648):

> " Si vacat ire viam neque te Bajovarius obstat,
> Qua vicina sedent Breonum loca, perge per Alpem,
> Ingrediens rapido qua gurgite volvitur Aenus.
> Inde Valentini benedicti templa require,
> Norica rura petens, ubi Byrrus vertitur undis."

CHAPTER XLII

FEVA, king of the Rugii, had given Favianis, one of
the few towns which remained on the bank of the
Danube, to his brother Ferderuchus. Near this
town, as I have related, Saint Severinus dwelt. When
Ferderuchus came, as was his wont, to pay his respects
to Severinus, the soldier of Christ began to tell him
eagerly of his approaching journey, and adjured him,
saying: "Know that I am to depart quickly to the
Lord. Therefore be warned, and beware of attempt-
ing, when I am gone, to lay hands on any of these
things which have been committed to me. Seize not
the substance of the poor and the captives. If thou
art guilty of such foolhardiness, which may Heaven
forfend, thou shalt feel the wrath of God!" Ferderuchus, perturbed by the unexpected admonition,
said, "Why dost thou adjure me and confound me?
I do not wish to be deprived of thy mighty protection.
Indeed, it is seemly that I should add something to thy
sacred bounty, which all men know, not take away
from it; that I may deserve to be protected by thy
wonted prayer, as was our father Flaccitheus. He
learned by experience that he was ever aided by the
merits of thy holiness." And Severinus said, "On
the very first opportunity thou wilt wish to violate
my cell. Then straightway thou shalt learn the
truth of my words, and be punished in a manner which
I do not desire." Then Ferderuchus promised that

he would observe the admonitions of the servant of Christ, and returned to his home.

But the kindly teacher did not cease to speak continually to his disciples, saying, " I trust in the grace of my Lord Jesus Christ that if ye persevere in his work, and in memory of me remain united in friendly association, he will give you the riches of eternal life, nor in this world will he deny you his consolation."

CHAPTER XLIII

ON the fifth of January he began to be slightly disquieted by a pain in the side.[1] When this persisted for three days, at midnight he commanded the brethren to be with him. He gave them instructions as to the disposal of his body, strengthened them with fatherly counsel, and bestowed upon them the following earnest and admirable discourse.

" Most beloved sons in Christ," he said, " ye know that blessed Jacob, when he was about to leave the world, and the time drew nigh that he must die, called unto his sons, and said, ' Gather yourselves together '; that he might tell them that which should befall them in the last days, and bless them every one according to his blessing.[2] But I am lowly and of lukewarm faith. I am inferior to such piety. I dare not assume the burden of this privilege. Yet there is one thing which is accordant with my humility, and which

---

[1] Pleurisy.　　　　　[2] Genesis, xlix, 1-33.

I will say. I will refer you to the examples of the elders, whose faith follow, considering the end of their conversation.[1] For Abraham, when called of the Lord, obeyed in faith. He went forth into a place which he was to receive into his possession; and he went forth not knowing whither he was to go. Therefore imitate the faith of this blessed patriarch, copy after his holiness, despise the things of earth, seek ever the heavenly home. Moreover I trust in the Lord, that eternal gain shall come to me from you. For I perceive that ye have enlarged my joy by the fervor of your spirit, that ye love justice, that ye cherish the bonds of brotherly love, that ye neglect not chastity, that ye guard the rule of humility. These things, so far as the eye of man hath power to see, I confidently praise and approve. But pray that those things which to human view are worthy, may be confirmed by the test of the eternal judgment; for God seeth not as man seeth. Indeed, as the divine word declareth, he searcheth all hearts, and understandeth all the imaginations of the thoughts.[2] Therefore constantly hope and pray for this, that God may enlighten the eyes of your understanding,[3] and open them, as blessed Elisha prayed, that ye may see [4] what hosts of saints surround and support you, what mighty aids are prepared for the faithful. For our God draws nigh to them that are without guile. Let the soldiers of God fail

[1] Hebrews, xiii, 7.

[2] I Chronicles, xxviii, 9; Romans, viii, 27.

[3] Ephesians, i, 18.   [4] II Kings, vi, 17.

not to pray without ceasing. Let him not be reluctant to repent, who was not ashamed to sin. Sinners, hesitate not to lament, if but by the overflowing of your tears the wrath of God may be appeased; for he hath seen fit to call a contrite spirit his sacrifice.[1] Therefore let us be humble in heart, tranquil in mind; guarding against all sins and ever mindful of the divine commands; knowing that meanness of garb, the name monk, the word religion, the outward form of piety, profiteth us not, if touching the observance of God's commands we be found degenerate and false. Therefore let your characters, my most beloved sons, accord with the vow which ye have assumed. It is a great crime to lead a sinful life, even for a man of this world;[2] how much more then for monks, who have fled from the enticements of the world as from a hideous wild beast, and have preferred Christ to all desires; whose gait and garb are held to be evidence of virtue ? But why, dearest sons, delay you further with a long address ? It remains to bestow upon you the last prayer of the blessed apostle, who saith, ' And now I commend you to God, and to the word of his grace, who is able to preserve you, and to give you an inheri-

---

[1] Psalms, li, 17.

[2] *Homo saecularis.* The same contrast of *saecularis* and *monachus* is made by Saint Jerome, *Epistola ad Paulinum de Institutione Monachi:* " Saecularium, et maxime potentium consortia devita. Quid tibi necesse est ea videre crebrius, quorum contemtu Monachus esse coepisti ? " *Opera* (Paris, 1693–1706), iv, 2, col. 566. *Homo saecularis* cannot here be rendered ' layman '; the monks themselves were reckoned laymen (*laici*) until the seventh century.

tance among all them which are sanctified.'[1] To him be the glory for ever and ever."

After this edifying address, he bade all in succession approach for his kiss. He received the sacrament of the communion; and altogether forbade that they should weep for him. Having stretched out his hand, and made the sign of the cross over his whole body, he commanded that they should sing a psalm. When the grief that overspread them kept them silent, he himself started the psalm, " Praise ye the Lord in his sanctuary; let everything that hath breath praise the Lord."[2] And so, on the eighth of January, repeating this verse, while we could hardly make the responses, he fell asleep in the Lord.

When he was buried, our elders, implicitly believing that, like his many other prophecies, what he had foretold in regard to our removal could not fail to come to pass, prepared a wooden casket;[3] that when the predicted migration of the people should take place, the commands of the prophet might be fulfilled.

[1] Acts, xx, 32.   [2] Psalms, cl, 1, 6.

[3] *Locellum:* in the next chapter, *loculum.* André Baudrillart, in his biography, *Saint Séverin, Apôtre du Norique* (Paris, 1908), p. 192, speaks of this coffin as " une sorte de chapelle portative ou d'oratoire," and represents the monks, throughout the removal to Italy, as ' praying and singing in it day and night.' This monstrous misconception may serve as a sufficient sample of the insouciance with which M. Baudrillart has performed his task.

CHAPTER XLIV

FERDERUCHUS was poor and ungodly, a greedy barbarian, and more greedy than the barbarians.   When
he learned of the death of Saint Severinus, he determined to carry off the clothing allotted to the poor,
and some other things.   Joining sacrilege to this crime,
he ordered that the silver goblet and the rest of the
altar service be carried off.   Since the service was on
the holy altars, the bailiff who was sent dared not
stretch out his hands to such a villainy, but compelled
a certain soldier, Avitianus by name, to commit the
robbery.   Although Avitianus executed the order un-.
willingly, he was from that moment plagued by an
incessant trembling in all his limbs, and furthermore
was possessed by a devil.   Therefore he quickly set
right his sins by adopting a better purpose.   For he
assumed the vow of the sacred profession, exchanged
the weapons of earth for those of heaven, and withdrew to a lonely isle.[1]

[1] Islands play an exceedingly large part in the history of monasticism in the Occident.   The islands of the Mediterranean, the isles of
Dalmatia and of the Tyrrhenian Sea, swarmed with monks: not to
mention other well-known examples.   Lucas Holstenius, *Codex Regu-
lorum Monasticorum* (Augustae Vindelicorum, 1759), i, p. ix; Sulpicius Severus, *De Beati Martini Vita*, vi, 5; Rutilius Namatianus, *De
Reditu suo*, i, 439–452 (Capraria: " Squalet lucifugis insula plena
viris "); Hilarius Arelatensis, *De Vita Sancti Honorati*, iii, 16, 17, in
Migne's *Patrologia Latina*, vol. l, coll. 1257 f. (Lerina).

The encircling watery barrier answered a threefold purpose.   It
served as protection alike against the enticements of the world, the
sword of the barbarian, and (according to the popular belief) the as-
saults of demons.

Ferderuchus, unmindful of the adjuration and prophecy of the holy man, seized all the possessions of the monastery, and left only the walls, which he could not carry across the Danube. But presently the threatened vengeance came upon him. For within the space of a month he was slain by Fredericus, his brother's son, and lost booty and life together.

Therefore King Odoacer waged war upon the Rugii. They were defeated, Fredericus was compelled to flee. His father Feva was taken prisoner, and removed to Italy with his wicked wife.[1]

Later, Odoacer heard that Fredericus had returned to his home. At once he dispatched a great army, under his brother Onoülfus; before whom Fredericus fled again, and went to King Theodoric, who was then at Novae,[2] a city of the province of Moesia.

Onoülfus, however, at his brother's command ordered all the Romans to migrate to Italy. Then all the inhabitants, led forth from the daily depredations of

---

[1] A long and entertaining account of a triumph celebrated by Odoacer at Rome after his victory, given by A. Thierry in his *Récits de l'Histoire Romaine au V* Siècle*, iii (Paris, 1860), pp. 352 ff., is purely a product of Thierry's luxuriant imagination. His invention is, however, unsuspectingly accepted as historical fact by Leopold von Ranke (*Weltgeschichte*, iv, 1, Leipsic, 1883, p. 377) and J. B. Bury (*The Later Roman Empire from Arcadius to Irene*, London, 1889, i, p. 289).

Paulus Diaconus (*De Gestis Langobardorum*, i, 19) says that Odoacer put Feletheus to death. As to Giso's fate we know nothing beyond what is declared by Eugippius. Thierry's statement (*Récits*, p. 353), followed by Bury (*Later Roman Empire*, i, p. 289), that she was " thrown into a dungeon," rests on no authority.

[2] Perhaps now Sistova, in Bulgaria.

the barbarians as from the house of Egyptian bondage, recognized the oracles of Saint Severinus.[1]

When Count Pierius compelled all to depart, the venerable Lucillus, then our priest, was not unmindful of the command of Severinus.   After he had ended singing with the monks the vesper psalms, he bade the place of burial to be opened.   When it was uncovered, a fragrance of such sweetness surrounded us who stood by, that we fell on the earth for joy and wonder.   Then whereas we reckoned in all human expectation to find the bones of his corpse disjoined, for the sixth year of his burial had already passed, we found the bodily structure intact.   For this miracle we returned unmeasured thanks to the Author of all, because the corpse of the saint, on which were no spices, which no embalmer's hand had touched, had staid unharmed, with beard and hair, even to that time.   Accordingly the linen cloths were changed; the corpse was inclosed in the casket that had been prepared for it long before, placed in a wagon drawn by horses, and presently carried forth.   All the provincials made the journey in our company.   They abandoned the towns on the banks of the Danube and were allotted the various

---

[1] Julius Jung (*Römer und Romaner in den Donauländern*, p. 205) believes that the exodus was less general than the words of Eugippius would seem to imply.   Whatever may have been the case with respect to the Roman population of Riverside Noricum, it is obvious that there was no general withdrawal from Noricum Mediterraneum, where the provincial organization was still in operation in the time of Theodoric.   Cassiodorus, *Variae*, iii, 50; Quitzmann, *Die älteste Geschichte der Baiern*, p. 123.

abodes of their exile through the different districts of Italy. So the body of the saint passed through many lands and was borne to a castle named Mount Feleter.[1]

CHAPTER XLV

DURING this time many that were attacked by divers diseases, and some who were oppressed by unclean spirits, experienced the instant healing of divine grace. A certain dumb man also was brought to this castle through the compassion of his kinsmen. He eagerly entered the oratory, where the body of the holy man still lay upon the wagon, and when he offered supplication behind the closed door of his mouth, in the chamber of his heart, immediately his tongue was loosed in prayer, and he spoke praise unto the Most High. And when he returned to the inn where he was wont to lodge, and was questioned as usual by nod and sign, he answered in a clear voice, that he had prayed and had offered praise to God. When he spoke, they who knew him were terrified and ran shouting to the oratory and told Saint Lucillus the priest, and us, who were with him and knew nothing of the event. Then we all rejoiced exceedingly, and returned thanks to the divine mercy.

[1] Probably the present Macerata di Monte Feltre, south of San Marino.

CHAPTER XLVI

BARBARIA, a lady of rank,[1] venerated Saint Severinus with pious devotion. She and her late husband had known him well by reputation and through correspondence. When, after the death of the saint, she heard that his body had with great labor been brought into Italy, and up to that time had not been committed to earth, she invited by frequent letters our venerable priest Marcianus, and also the whole brotherhood. Then with the authorization of Saint Gelasius, pontiff of the Roman see, and received by the people of Naples with reverent obsequies, the body was laid to rest by the hands of Saint Victor the bishop in the Lucullan castle,[2] in a mausoleum which Barbaria had built.[3]

[1] Thomas Hodgkin (*Italy and her Invaders*, iii, Oxford, 1885, pp. 190 f. ; or 2d ed., 1896, pp. 172 f.) seeks to identify Barbaria with the widow of Orestes and mother of Romulus Augustulus. On this point see Jung's *Römer und Romaner in den Donauländer*, p. 134; and Max Büdinger's *Eugipius, eine Untersuchung*, in *Sitzungsberichte der kaiserlichen Akademie der Wissenschaften* (Vienna), philosophisch-historische Classe, xci, 1 (1878), pp. 802 f.

[2] Now Pizzofalcone.

[3] Two more translations still awaited the body. October 14, 903, the Lucullan castle was abandoned through fear of the marauding Saracens. The remains of the saint were borne in solemn procession to the great Benedictine monastery of Saint Severinus, within the walls of Naples. Joannes Diaconus Neapolitanus, *Martyrium Sancti Procopii*, in Octavius Cajetanus's *Vitae Sanctorum Siculorum* (Panormi, 1657), ii, p. 62, reprinted in L. A. Muratori's *Rerum Italicarum Scriptores* (Mediolani, 1723–51), i, 2, pp. 271 f.; and the same, printed

At this solemnity many afflicted by divers diseases, whom it would be tedious to enumerate, were instantly healed. Among them was a venerable handmaid of

from another manuscript, under the title of *Translatio Sancti Severini* or *Historia Translationis*, in *Acta Sanctorum*, January, i (1643), pp. 1100–1103, and reprinted thence in *Monumenta Germaniae Historica: Scriptores Rerum Langobardicarum et Italicarum* Saec. VI–IX (Hannoverae, 1878), pp. 452–459. — It should be noted, however, that Luigi Parascandolo, in his *Memorie Storiche-Critiche-Diplomatiche della Chiesa di Napoli* (Naples, 1847–51), ii, pp. 253 f., doubts the authenticity of this narrative, which, he thinks, owes at least its present form to the labor of some Benedictine monk living in the monastery of Saint Severinus at the time of the revival of learning.— Descriptions of the monastery, now for the most part secularized and occupied by the Royal Neapolitan State Archives, and of the church of Saints Severinus and Sosius connected with it, may be found in *Napoli e i Luoghi Celebri delle sue Vicinanze* (Naples, 1845), i, pp. 233–243, and in the current guidebooks.

Here the remains of Severinus reposed for many centuries, not in the large church, but beneath the great altar of the smaller primitive church, or chapel, connected with it. The inscription on the great altar is given in *Acta Sanctorum*, January, i, p. 499:

> "Hic duo sancta simul divinaque corpora Patres
> Sosius unanimes et Severinus habent."

According to Sebastian Brunner (*Leben des St. Severin*, Vienna, 1879, p. 170), the following inscription was found in the crypt when it was opened in 1807: "Divis Severino Noricorum in Oriente Apostolo et Sosio Levitae B. Januarii Episcopi in Passione socio Templum ubi eorum SS. Corpora sub Altare majori requiescunt et Apostolico indultu cum oblatione sacra purgantes animae liberantur."

The fourth removal was on May 30, 1807, after the dissolution of the monastery under the French domination, to the town of Fratta Maggiore, a few miles north of Naples. Stanislao d'Aloe, in *Napoli e i Luoghi Celebri delle sue Vicinanze*, i, p. 240 (d'Aloe errs as to the date); G. A. Galante, *Memorie dell' Antico Cenobio Lucullano di S. Severino Abate* (Naples, 1869), p. 41; Brunner, *St. Severin*, pp. 167–

God, Processa by name, a citizen of Naples, who suffered from a severe and troublesome sickness. Invited by the virtues of the holy corpse, she hastened to meet it on the way; and when she approached the vehicle in which the venerable body was borne, immediately she was free from sickness in all her members.

Also at that time a blind man, Laudicius, was startled when he heard the unexpected clamor of the people singing psalms, and anxiously asked his household what it was. When they replied that the body of a certain Saint Severinus was passing, he was moved by the spirit, and asked that he be led to the window; from which one possessed of sight could behold afar

172. There was, it would appear from Brunner's account, some ecclesiastical as well as civil authority for the removal of the remains. Nevertheless Dr. Galante considers that they were " fraudolentemente rapitoci " (p. 41), and in his dissertation (pp. 41 f.) strongly urges their return to Naples. " Cives Fractenses," he writes me under date of March 20, 1914, " non S. Severini, sed S. Sosii corpus repetebant, et occasionem nacti expulsionis Monachorum e coenobio et templo Severinianio, prope Archivium Magnum, corpora utriusque simul quiescentia rapuerunt, et ad oppidum suum transtulerunt, ubi nunc in majori templo Fractensi quiescunt. Quamvis Monachi postea redierint, haud curae fuit, sacra lipsana repetere. Superioribus annis ego nullum non movi lapidem ut corpus S. Severini Neapoli restitueretur, sed frustra; praecordia tantum sanguine intincta, et quatuor ossa restituta sunt, quae nunc in templo S. Severini asservantur."

From 1807 to 1874 the bodies of Severinus and Sosius lay in a small chapel near the parish church of Fratta Maggiore. They were then removed into the church, to a new chapel, where the coffins, placed on either side the altar, were covered with red velvet, and distinguished by the gilt letters S. S. M. (Sanctus Sosius Martyr) and S. S. A. (Sanctus Severinus Abbas). Brunner, *St. Severin*, pp. 179 f.

off the multitude singing psalms and the carriage bearing the sacred body. And when he leaned forth from the window and prayed, straightway he saw, and pointed out his acquaintances and neighbors one by one. Thereupon all who heard him wept for joy and returned thanks to God.

Marinus too, precentor of the holy church at Naples, could not recover his health after a terrible sickness, and suffered from a constant headache. In faith he leaned his head against the carriage, and immediately lifted it up free from pain. In memory of this benefit, he always came on the anniversary of the saint's burial and rendered to God thanks and the sacrifice of a vow.

I have related three of the numberless miracles which were wrought on the arrival of the saint through his mediation and virtues. Let it suffice; though many know of more.

A monastery, built at the same place to the memory of the blessed man, still endures. By his merits many possessed with devils have received and do receive healing through the effective grace of God; to whom is honor and glory for ever and ever. Amen.

Illustrious minister of Christ, thou hast the memoir. From it make by thy editorial care a profitable work.

LETTER OF PASCHASIUS TO EUGIPPIUS

PASCHASIUS the deacon to the holy and ever most beloved priest Eugippius.

Dearest brother in Christ, thou measurest me by the measure of thy skill, eloquence, and happy leisure, and disdainest to consider my vexatious employments and manifold imperfections. Yet through the contemplation of thy love I sustain the injury to my modesty.[1]

Thou hast sent me a memoir to which the eloquence of the trained writer can add nothing, and in a short compendium hast produced a work which the whole church can read. The life and character of Saint Severinus, who dwelt in the provinces bordering on the Pannonias, thou hast portrayed with much faithfulness; and thou hast handed down to the memory of future generations, to remain through long ages, the miracles which divine virtue hath wrought through him. The deeds of the good cannot perish with time. All persons to whom thy narrative shall bring Saint Severinus shall have him before them, and shall perceive that in a certain sense he dwells with them. And

---

[1] Paschasius here imitates Sulpicius Severus, *De Beati Martini Vita*, Praef., 1: " Quid enim esset, quod non amori tuo vel cum detrimento mei pudoris inpenderem ? "

so as thou hast told very simply, and explained very clearly, these particulars which thou didst ask me to narrate, I have thought it best not to try to make any addition to thy work. Indeed, it is one thing to relate what we have been told, quite another thing, to draw from the stores of our own experience. The virtues of teachers are particularly visible in their daily life, and consequently are more easily depicted by their pupils. By God's gift inspired, thou understandest the value of the deeds of the saints for the improvement of the minds of the good: their profitableness, the fervor they impart, their cleansing power. On this point we have the authority of the well-known words of the apostle, " being ensamples to the flock; " [1] and Saint Paul commanded Timothy, " be thou an example of the believers." [2] For this reason Saint Paul compiles a concise catalogue of the just, and, beginning from Abel, recounts the virtues of distinguished men. [3] So also that most faithful Mattathias, as the days drew near that he should die a glorious death, distributed to his sons as an inheritance the examples of the saints; [4] that fired with sacred zeal by the wonderful battles of the saints, they might hold their lives as naught in the defense of the eternal laws. Nor did the sons find the father's teaching false. For so greatly did the deeds of the elders profit them, that with most manifest faith they terrified armed princes, overcame the camps of the wicked, overthrew far and

---

[1] I Peter, v, 3.
[2] I Timothy, iv, 12.
[3] Hebrews, xi.
[4] I Maccabees, ii, 49 seq.

wide the worship and altars of demons,[1] and decorated
with perennial garlands they provided a civic crown for
their glorious country.

For this reason also I rejoice that through a brother's service something is provided for the ornaments
of the bride of Christ;[2] not that at any time, as I
believe, have there been lacking illustrious examples of
the elders, but because it is fitting that the palace of
the Great King should have the standards of many
victories. For true virtue is not obscured by the
multitude of virtues, but yearns for their increase, and
is enlarged thereby.[3]

[1] I Maccabees, iii, 8; v, 44, 68; x, 83 f.
[2] Revelation, xxi, 2, 9.
[3] " As one lamp lights another nor grows less,
So nobleness enkindles nobleness."

APPENDIX

I

A List of Editions and Translations of the Life

(a) *Editions*

Laurentius Surius, in *De Probatis Sanctorum Historiis*, vol. i (Coloniae Agrippinae, 1570), pp. 153–161. Printed from a greatly abridged manuscript, now lost. Lacks the letters and the table of chapters; chapters 6, 13, 14, 16, 18–31, 39, 42; and parts of chapters 4, 9, 11, 12, 17, and 43.[1] Repeated in the editions of 1576 (*ibid.*), i, pp. 159–167, and 1581 (Venetiis), i, ff. 49–52. The third Cologne edition of Surius, published under the title *Vitae Sanctorum* (1617) repeats (i, pp. 111–121) Velserus's text of 1595, with the addition of the letter of Eugippius to Paschasius.

The latest edition of Surius (Augustae Taurinorum, 1875–80) reproduces the mutilated text of the earliest editions. Tom. i, pp. 137–150.

Caesar Baronius, *Annales Ecclesiastici*, tom. vi (Romae, 1595), first printed the letter of Paschasius to Eugippius (*a.* 496) and that part of the letter of Eugippius to Paschasius which relates to the native country of Severinus (*a.* 454); also chapters 18, 19, and 42. Baronius

---

[1] There is a very curious bias displayed in some of the omissions. These include the descriptions of the habits and daily life of Severinus (4, 39); the rehabilitation of the repentant husbandman (12); and the exhortation to the monks to lead lives of practical godliness (43).

had the Life complete in manuscript, and printed nearly a third of it in the Annals under the years 454, 473, 475, 482, 488, 493, 496.[1] These portions are repeated in the subsequent editions of his work, of which there are ten or more.

Marcus Velserus. *Historia ab Eugippio ante Annos circiter MC. scripta, qua Tempora, quae Attilae mortem consequuta sunt, occasione vitae S. Severini illustrantur. Ex Bibliotheca S. Emmerani Reginoburg. nunc primum edita, cum scholiis.* Augustae Vindelicorum, 1595. Without the letter of Eugippius and the table of chapters. The first separate edition. Repeated in Velserus's *Opera* (*ibid.*, 1682), pp. 629–676.

Henricus Canisius, *Antiqua Lectio*, tom. vi (Ingolstadii, 1604), first printed entire the letter of Eugippius to Paschasius. This is found in the second edition of Canisius, by Jacques Basnage (*Thesaurus Monumentorum*, etc., Amstelaedami, 1725), in vol. i, pp. 411 f.

Joannes Bolland, in *Acta Sanctorum*, Januarius, tom. i (Antverpiae, 1643), pp. 483–499; editio novissima, tom. i (Parisiis, etc., 1863), pp. 483–499.

---

[1] A table of the chapters of the Life printed by Baronius may be of service. The first column gives the year of the Annals; the second, the sections, which are found in several of the editions; the third, page references to tom. viii (1751) of the best edition, that of Lucca; the fourth, the chapters of the Life.

454	25–31	168 ff.	1, 2; part of the letter of Eugippius.
	33, 34	170 f.	3
473	3–9	318 ff.	5, 8, 11 (2d paragraph).
475	4	331	7
	35	338	18
482	53–63	414–417	19, 40, 42, 43 (omitting the address), 44 (2 paragraphs).
488	9–15	504 f.	44 (completion), 45
493	3	554	32 (the prophecy only).
496	49–52	606 f.	46; the letter of Paschasius.

Hieronymus Pez, in *Scriptores Rerum Austriacarum*, tom. i (Lipsiae, 1721), coll. 64-93.

Berthold Rizel, in *Sancta et Beata Austria* (Augustae Vindelicorum, 1750), pp. 71-124. Repeated from Pez.

Joseph Resch, in *Annales Ecclesiae Sabionensis nunc Brixinensis atque Conterminarum* (Augustae Vindelicorum, 1760), tom. i, pp. 296-322. A number of chapters toward the end are abbreviated.

Johann Heinrich von Falckenstein, in *Geschichten des grossen Herzogthums und ehemaligen Königreichs Bayern*, part i (Munich, etc.,1763), pp. 79-120.

Anton Albert Muchar, in *Das römische Norikum*, vol. ii (Grätz, 1826), pp. 152-239. Repeated from Pez.

Jacques Paul Migne, in *Patrologiae Cursus Completus*, vol. lxii (Parisiis, 1848), coll. 1167-1200. Repeated from *Acta Sanctorum*. The letter of Paschasius is in the same volume, coll. 39 f.

Anton Kerschbaumer. *Vita S. Severini, auctore Eugippio, secundum Codicem antiquissimum, qui Romae asservatur. Cum tabula specimen codicis Lateranensis continente.* Scaphusiae, 1862. The first edition to contain the table of chapters.

Johann Friedrich, in *Kirchengeschichte Deutschlands*, vol. i (Bamberg, 1867), pp. 431-489.

Hermann Sauppe. *Eugippii Vita Sancti Severini.* Berolini, 1877. In *Monumenta Germaniae Historica*, Auctores Antiquissimi, tom. i, pars ii.

Pius Knoell. *Eugippii Vita Sancti Severini.* Vindobonae, 1886. In *Corpus Scriptorum Ecclesiasticorum Latinorum*, vol. viii, pars ii.

Theodor Mommsen. *Eugippii Vita Severini.* Berolini, 1898. In *Scriptores Rerum Germanicarum in usum Scholarum ex Monumentis Germaniae Historicis recusi.*

(b) *German Translations*

Johannes a Via. *Das Leben des H. Severini Nortgowischen Apostels, durch Eugippium beschriben.* In his *Historien der Lieben Heiligen Gottes, aus dem Latein* [of Surius] *verteutschet* (Munich, 1574–80), vol. i, ff. xciv–xcix.

Mathias Fuhrmann. *Leben und Wunderthaten des Heiligen Nordgauer, oder Oesterreicher Apostels Severin.* Vienna, 1746.

Johann Heinrich von Falckenstein, 1763, in columns parallel to his text.

Leben des heil. Severin, aus dem Latein. Passau, 1817.

P. Durach. *Das Leben des h. Severin.* Passau, 1847.

Carl Ritter. *Das Leben des heiligen Mönches und Apostels der Noriker Severin, beschrieben von Eugippius.* Linz, 1853.

Jakob Leitner, in *Leben und Wirken des Hl. Severin und der heiligen Bischöfe Maximilian und Valentin* (3d edition, Passau, 1868), pp. 112–174.

Karl Rodenberg. *Leben des heiligen Severin, von Eugippius.* Leipsic, 1878; 2d edition, 1884. In *Geschichtschreiber der deutschen Vorzeit.*

Sebastian Brunner. *Das Leben des Noriker-Apostels St. Severin, von seinem Schüler Eugippius. Die wichtigste Urkunde aus der Zeit der Völkerwanderung. Aus dem Lateinischen. Mit Einleitung, Erklärungen, möglichst vollständiger Literatur und einem Bericht über die Grabestätten St. Severins bis auf die neueste Zeit. Mit einer Abbildung der neuen St. Severinuskirche in Wien.* Vienna, 1879.

(c) *French Translation* [1]

In Jean Baptiste Carnandet's *Les Actes des Saints*, Janvier, iii (Lyons, 1867), pp. 481–509.

II

A LATIN HYMN IN PRAISE OF SAINT SEVERINUS [2]

Canticum laudis domino canentes
Hunc diem festum celebremus omnes,
Quo Severinus penetravit almus
  Celsa polorum.
Quis stilo dives modulansque plectro
Cuncta signorum replicare possit,
Quae potens Christus studiis opimis
  Contulit ejus ?

---

[1] Tillemont, whose accuracy is commonly unimpeachable, says of the Life (*Memoires pour servir a l'Histoire Ecclesiastique des six Premiers Siècles*, Paris, 1701–12, xvi, p. 180) " Elle est traduite en françois dans les Saints illustres de Mr. d'Andilli." A careful search, however, has so far failed to reveal such a translation. The reference to it in Remy Ceillier's *Histoire Générale des Auteurs Sacrés et Ecclesiastiques* (Paris, 1729–63), xvi, p. 158, may be borrowed from Tillemont.

[2] A remarkable Neapolitan hymnary, apparently that of the monastery of Saint Severinus, is preserved in two closely related manuscripts of about the end of the tenth century, Codex Vaticanus 7172 and MS. 1092 of the Bibliothèque Nationale at Paris. Guido Maria Dreves has printed it from these, under the title of *Hymnarius Severinianus*, as volume xiv a of *Analecta Hymnica Medii Aevi* (Leipsic, 1893). In it are two hymns (34 and 35, in Dreves's edition) in praise of Saint Severinus. The second dates from the tenth century, as is shown by its reference to the signs and wonders that accompanied the translation of the relics of the saint from the Lucullan castle to Naples. It contains nothing of biographical interest. The other was first published by Antoine Frédéric Ozanam, in his *Documents Inédits pour servir a l'Histoire Littéraire de l'Italie* (Paris, 1850), pp. 241 ff., from the

Inclitus vates nimiumque felix,
Saepius cui deus intimabat   (11, 39,
Tunc ad oppressi populi salutem   40)
    Multa futura,
Voce praesaga laqueos latronum   (10)
Atque praedonum machinas retexens   (4, 5)
Valde tutabat monitis supernis   (11, 25, 30)
    Oppida fessa.
Dulce solamen miseris ministrans
Horridam pestem famis amputavit,   (3, 18)
Barbara plures feritate victos   (8, 9, 10, 19)
    Solvit ab hoste.
Magne confessor, humilis magister,   (36)
Tu quidem normam monachis dedisti,   (4, 9, 39)
Calle demonstrans sobrio sequaces
    Scandere celum.

Vatican manuscript. It is Ozanam's opinion that it was composed shortly after the preparation of the Life. The classical purity of form and the unblurred outline of the story strongly support this view. After Ozanam, Migne, Sauppe, Knoell, and Mommsen, in their editions of the Life, and Dreves (as above) have printed the hymn. Dreves alone has used the Paris manuscript. He has also supplied, from another hymn with a similar ending, the last three lines of the final stanza, the Doxology, which is incomplete in the manuscripts. His text is, however, carelessly printed. André Baudrillart gives a French translation as an appendix to his *Saint Séverin* (1908). Sebastian Brunner in his translation of the Life (1879), pp. 181 f., gives in German a very free metrical paraphrase, " so arranged," he says, " that it might be sung as a church hymn on the festival of the saint." Its suitability for this purpose is lessened by the fact that Brunner has inadvertently substituted ' Silenus ' for ' Silvinus ' in his rendering of the ninth stanza.

    The text which is here presented follows that of Mommsen, with some correction of punctuation, and with the completing verses of the Doxology from Dreves. The marginal numerals in parentheses refer to chapters of the Life.

In tuis sacris manibus refulsit   (13)
Celitus lumen, refluensque crevit
Ad tuos haustus olei liquamen   (28)
    Fontis ad instar.
Condolens cunctos inopes fovebat,   (17)
Languidos sanans relevabat aegros: (6, 14,
Omnis accedens salubrem medelam   33, 34, 38,
    Sumpsit ab illo.   39)
Tuque Sylvinum loculo jacentem,   (16)
Fratribus coram precibus peractis,
Morte devicta redire fecisti ad
    Gaudia vitae.
Cereos flamma fidei cremante   (11)
Arguit sanctus pater infideles:
Nosque flammescunt deitatis igne
    Algida corda.
Cujus ad funus veniens sacratum
Mutus accepit modulos loquelae,   (45)
Caecus exultat procul ambulantes   (46)
    Cernere notos.
Neapolis, gaude redimita festa,
Plaude caelestem retinens patronum,
Quem tibi summus decus et juvamen
    Praestitit auctor.
Hujus o clemens meritis creator
Gloriam nobis veniamque confer,
Quo tui cultus super astra semper
    Luce fruamur.
Gloriam patri resonemus omnes,
Gloriam Christo supplices canamus,
Cum quibus sanctus simul et creator
    Spiritus regnat.

Translation

Singing a song of praise unto the Lord, let us all celebrate this festal day, on which kind Severinus entered the heights of heaven.

What eloquent pen, what tuneful lyre can repeat all the miracles which mighty Christ bestowed upon his excellent zeal ?

Seer of renown and exceeding good omen, to whom, for the salvation of the people then prostrate, God often made known many things that were to come,

With prophetic word he unravelled the snares of robbers and the tricks of plunderers, and by supernal warnings strongly defended the exhausted towns.

Giving sweet relief to the unfortunate, he banished the horrid curse of famine, and set free from the foe many who had been conquered by the fierce barbarians.

Great confessor, meek master, thou didst indeed give a pattern to the monks, showing them how to mount to heaven, following in the narrow path of temperance.

In thy sacred hands glittered the light from heaven; and the oil at thy drawing overflowed and increased like a fountain.

He sympathized with all the destitute, and cherished them; he healed the sick, he relieved the suffering: every one who approached received healing remedy.

And in the presence of the brethren thou didst pray over Silvinus as he lay in the coffin, and, conquering death, bring him back to the joys of life.

By the flame that burned the waxen tapers of the faithful the holy father convicted the unbelievers; and our cold hearts flame with the fire of God.

Coming to his sacred burial, the dumb received speech, the blind exulteth to recognize those that walk afar.

Naples, rejoice in thy festal crown!   Clap thy hands, keeping the heavenly patron whom the sovereign Author hath bestowed upon thee as thy honor and help.

For his merits, O merciful Creator, grant us glory and pardon, that above the stars we may ever enjoy the light of thy worship.

Let us all resound glory to the Father, let us in suppliance sing glory unto Christ; with whom reigneth the Holy Spirit and Creator.

III

CHRONOLOGICAL TABLE

(Numerals in parentheses refer to chapters of the Life.)

453. Death of Attila.   At about this time Severinus comes " from the parts of the East to the marches of Riverside Noricum and the Pannonias " (1).

455, 9 Sept.   Sabaria is destroyed by an earthquake (2 ?).

476, 23 Aug.   Odoacer is proclaimed ruler of Italy.
28 Aug.   The patrician Orestes is " unjustly slain." (Letter to Paschasius).
Autumn or winter ?   Primenius takes refuge with Severinus (*ibid.*).

c. 482, 8 Jan. Death of Severinus at his monastery near Favianis (43).

487. Odoacer wages war on the Rugii.   Fredericus flees. Feletheus and Giso are removed to Italy (44).

488 ? Fredericus returns.   He is again put to flight, this time by an army which Odoacer sends under his brother Onoülfus.   Onoülfus and Count Pierius

order the Roman provincials of Riverside Noricum to withdraw to Italy. The body of Severinus is disinterred, and is accompanied by the monks to Mount Feleter, in Italy. The provincials are assigned abodes "through the different districts of Italy" (44).

Fredericus goes to Theodoric, king of the Ostrogoths, at Novae in Moesia (44).

489. Theodoric, with the authorization of the Emperor Zeno, invades Italy, and defeats Odoacer at the Isonzo (28 Aug.) and at Verona (30 Sept.). Fulfillment of the prophecy of Severinus (32).

492–96. Gelasius is pope. Sometime during his pontificate, the body of Severinus is removed to the Lucullan castle, near Naples, and there placed by Saint Victor, bishop of Naples, in a mausoleum built for it by Barbaria (46).

493, 27 Feb. Peace between Theodoric and Odoacer. 15 Mar. Odoacer is assassinated by Theodoric, who becomes sole ruler of Italy.

511. Eugippius, second abbot of the monastery of Saint Severinus at the Lucullan castle, sends the Life of Severinus to Deacon Paschasius.

526, 30 Aug. Death of Theodoric.

INDEX OF AUTHORS CITED
IN THE NOTES

GENERAL INDEX

Lightning Source UK Ltd.
Milton Keynes UK
UKHW030121070821
388442UK00007B/1515